POWER & PRIVILEGE

Their Abuse in the World

Mini Sarla

Published by Winmark Communications
Glendale, AZ 85308
www.winmarkcom.com

ISBN: 978-0-615-41071-5

www.winmarkcom:com/powerandprivilege.htm

Copy Editors:
Jeanette Chaplin (jeanettechaplin@yahoo.com),
Mary L Holden (maryholdeneditor.com)

Proceeds from the sale of this book will go to charity.

Printed and bound in the United States of America

Dedicated to

My mother and the memory of my father

Hope

Cast not the hope this book brings
Cast it with yours or it shall sing
Cast-up woes of a soul left mute
Cast aside but absurdly resolute

– Mini Sarla

FOREWORD

"At long last a book that touches upon every aspect of life and the pervasive abuses of power and privilege in the world. Mini Sarla manages to reveal not only the subtle abuses that lurk in our midst, but also the overt, in a refreshingly enlightened and non-confrontational way that appeals to the higher conscience of the reader. It should be read both by the victims of abuse as well as the perpetrators.

"The book starts by highlighting how the human race is tilting the balance of survival in its favor to such an extreme, and how modern society seems to have lost sight of compassion, all in the name of modernization and progress.

"Mini then leads the reader literally from womb to tomb and beyond, to highlight where and how abuses of power and privilege occur, and the adverse effects they have on the psyche of society. She engages the reader by constantly raising questions that hopefully will result in the inner awakening that is woefully needed in our troubled times."

-Zerbanoo Gifford

◊   International Woman of the Year–2006
◊   A former director of Anti-Slavery International
◊   Author, human rights campaigner, and founder of the ASHA Foundation and Centre
◊   Pioneer for Asian women in British politics; she chaired the Commission, *Looking into ethnic minority involvement in*
◊   *British Life* and was a member of the advisory group to the British Home Secretary

ACKNOWLEDGMENTS

I would like to thank all the people who contributed to *Wikipedia.com, The Free Encyclopedia*—an encyclopedia FOR THE PEOPLE BY THE PEOPLE.

For her invaluable input, my heartfelt gratitude goes to my friend Kusoom Vadgama. My gratitude also goes to Bruce Marion, Lee Smith, Michael Bruno, Bill, Dorothy, Barbara, Cathy, Lisa, and Charlotte.[1]

I would also like to thank Malinda for her contribution to the preparation of this manuscript.

---

[1]Some of the individuals chose not to have their full names printed.

Judgments

I've watched and judged all through life.
The judgments of missing human grace
Leave me to despair.
The wise monk advised letting go,
But I pounded them onto the keyboard instead,
And hope they spread through cyberspace.

– Mini Sarla

CONTENTS

INTRODUCTION

This is a book about two societal characteristics—power and privilege—and their influence in the world. The description of these two characteristics are based mainly on childhood experiences in India and as an adult in the United States, as well as information shared by friends and colleagues from various parts of the world.

The book addresses not only some of the more pervasive trends in society, but the potential for abuse in the future. The material presented has been substantiated by data available on the Internet, specifically *Wikipedia.com, The Free Encyclopedia.* The liberal use of references *directly* from *Wikipedia* served the purpose of acknowledging the contributions of countless average individuals and, more important, supporting their selfless and collaborative effort. It also served the purpose of escaping the elitism of academia and the monopolies of the established power brokers and reaching out to the average and often abused person.[2] Material was also taken from newspapers, magazines, books, television and documentaries.

---

[2]Mike Adams, "Mainstream Media Criticizes Wikipedia because it Represents a Decentralization of their Information Monopoly." Natural-News.com, Natural Health, Natural Living, Natural News. 15 Jan. 2007. Web. 24 Sept. 2010.
http://www.naturalnews.com/021420_wikipedia_mainstream_media.html.

Homo sapiens [Latin: "wise man"], or the human race, bestowed with a superior intellect, erect posture and opposable thumb, stands unrivaled against any other species on the planet. Humans enjoy a special status, which over the millennia has evolved and acquired new dimensions, not only through natural selection and the survival of the fittest, but also through civilization.

Most of the successes of modern civilization are driven by various societal institutions, which include religion, culture, tradition, formal education, agriculture, commerce and trade. These institutions have a positive influence on life, in general, and impart a semblance of purpose and order. For example, most people abide by the law, attend school, worship God, get an education, acquire skills, get a job and get married.

However, these institutions also create hierarchies that allow humans to enjoy a more privileged status than other life forms on the planet. Some of the institutions have such a strong hold on society that they grant more power and privilege to select individuals over other fellow humans.

In modern civilization, order in society is largely dependent on individual conscience. Order is also preserved by rewarding conformity and punishing nonconformity to the prevailing laws and customs. Barring the very basic physiologic needs, such as satisfying hunger, conformity is designed to make people do what they would instinctively be less inclined to do. The military is the best example of rigid adherence to conformity. Take the simple example of a military parade: a large group of humans dressed in identical clothes, marching in unison, in perfect geometric formation, at elaborate ceremonies with bands and fanfare, either saluting pieces of colorful fabric hoisted on tall poles, or saluting a decorated fellow human, called a commander, who enjoys a particularly privileged status and wields considerable power.

Organized religion (as opposed to individual spirituality and faith in the Divine) is another preeminent societal institution that influences human behavior. Religious indoctrination feeds on fear which is then used to manipulate the human mind and behavior to such extremes that it can destroy even the most basic survival instincts and logic, often leading humans to horrific deaths, including those encountered in holy wars, genocide, suicide missions, or self-immolation.

In most religions, God is always assigned a male gender: He, our Lord and Master, His Kingdom, and never as female. Another way in which almost every organized religion affects human behavior is through the teaching that "man"—not woman—is the highest form of Divine Creation in the Universe, or that "men"—not women—are created in the image of God. Considering the size of the planet Earth in the solar system, a miniscule part of the Milky Way Galaxy surrounded by hundreds of billions of similar galaxies, in a seemingly endless Universe, these particular religious beliefs seem like quantum leaps of faith. Some religions promote the revelations of wise men who say they hear the voice of God as divine dictum; others involve the worship of idols portraying diverse aspects of the Divine in various supernatural human male and female forms. A few religions even promise their virtuous and compliant men a paradise full of comforts and rewards.

Little wonder that humans, especially the men, believe they are the most privileged species, superior to all other life forms on the planet, not only in intellect, but also in body and spirit. Does this perception of superiority impart a sense of power and privilege in the world today? If so, how and where is it manifest?

The abuse of power and privilege has become so pervasive that it is beginning to have a detrimental effect on society as a whole. The problem is compounded by the current geopolitical trends driven by individual and corporate greed threatening modern civilization. Recent events such as the crash of the global financial markets, which sent the U.S. on a tail spin into the Great Recession of 2008–2009, have piqued the interest of the normally complacent and silent majority who spend most of their days working hard to keep food on the table and a roof over their head. The time for "business as usual" may be over.

This book urges readers not only to re-examine the established norms but also to look beyond the overt to cope with the ills plaguing society today. Individuals who no longer have jobs or cannot satisfy their basic needs, or are adversely affected by these abusive trends would be particularly served by reading this book. Now more than ever before, it is morally imperative for people to be informed and voice their concerns.

An attempt is made here to isolate and illustrate select areas of modern civilization where power is abused by a small but significant number of individuals or groups of individuals to the detriment of the vast majority.

It particularly serves to raise the awareness of the unsuspecting majority to abuses that are not always willful, nor always imposed on unwilling members of society, but accepted as the norm. The book is not merely intended to put down the powerful and those who may be so privileged. On the contrary, it is designed to raise the awareness of the abused and the abusers alike.

Modern society is ripe for triggers that may start a moral domino effect through-out the world so that it can be saved from the ravages of the power wielded by immoral, bigoted, greed-driven, corrupt and often violently abusive minority in our midst. This book serves to be one such trigger. Fairness must be brought back to all segments of society—it must form the foundation for a peaceful transformation to an enlightened world and a better life for all.

Fortunately, there are enlightened powerful and privileged people who give generously to the disadvantaged, and who support research and development for the good of society.[3] Without their charitable and philanthropic contributions, the world would be much worse off.

---

[3] "List of wealthiest charitable foundations," *Wikipedia, The Free Encyclopedia.* Wikipedia, The Free Encyclopedia. 24 June 2010. Web. 19 Sept. 2010. http://en.wikipedia.org/wiki/

Chapter 1
The Power and Privilege of Being Human

A human being is a part of the whole called the Universe, a part limited in time and space. He experiences himself, his thoughts and feelings as something separated from the rest, a kind of optical delusion of his consciousness. This delusion is a kind of prison for us, restricting us to our personal desires and to affection for a few persons nearest to us. Our task must be to free ourselves from this prison by widening our circle of compassion to embrace all living creatures and the whole of nature in its beauty.

– Albert Einstein (1879–1955)
German-Swiss theoretical physicist,
Awarded Nobel Prize in Physics in 1921

Directly or indirectly, for better or for worse, humans affect all other life forms on this planet. In Nature's food chain, where does *Homo sapiens* belong? Most humans would imagine themselves at the helm. But, where would humans be if left in the elements? Without the tools afforded by civilization, or the omnipresent food markets, where would they really be in the food chain? No longer endowed with fangs or claws, they would be herbivores living in constant fear of being devoured by carnivores. Imagine what the human life span and the world human population would be with a return to such "natural" circumstances.

7

The Food Chain

With civilization and the division of labor, the food chain is skewed in favor of humans. Today, they do not have to grow their own fruits and vegetables, or go hunting for their next meal, if they choose not to. With the advent of trade and commerce, food is made available on demand, bringing an endless variety of food products to households in urban dwellings. Over time, this has led to the formation of a booming global food industry with the creation of huge cooperative farms where genetically modified plants and animals are raised and where animal husbandry is applied with great success. What could be wrong with such a successful application of human ingenuity? On close examination, it becomes obvious that compassion toward animals raised in large cooperative farms is woefully lacking. Except for feeding them, the privileged humans pay little attention to any of the other needs of these helpless creatures, such as the freedom to roam and graze. They stand day after day in cramped dens, often knee deep in their excrement.[4] On poultry farms the birds are jam-packed in sheds where they are literally piled on top of each other.[5] These animals are not pests but a source of food.

What purpose do such cruel practices serve? Is it simply a case of efficiency to make food more affordable or to eliminate world

---

[4] *Dairy and Veal.* Mercy for Animals. Web. 10 Sept 2010.
http://www.mercyforanimals.org/dairy_and_veal.asp

[5] *Poultry.* Mercy for Animals. Web. 10 Sept 2010.
http://www.mercyforanimals.org/poultry.asp

hunger? Or is there more to the scenario? If one analyzes the modern food chain starting from the farmer to the manufacturer of packaged food, and then on to the distributor, the retailer and the omnipresent consumer, the answer becomes obvious. It all boils down to profits. And who makes the most profit in this modern food chain? Among the highest profit margins are the privileges of the powerful corporations that manufacture packaged goods. And chief among them are the multinational corporations who wield substantial power over all the others in the chain, including the consumer because their products enjoy brand name recognition and global market shares. As a result, the maximum profit margins are realized by such corporations. Does the wealth so generated go to the shareholders? Not always, as one might expect. Such profits go to pay the top executives' salary packages [more on this in Chapter 4]. Meanwhile, everyone else is at the mercy of the so-called market forces.

The most disadvantaged in this food chain are the individual farmers who are the source of the food. They are constantly squeezed to produce more food for less money. And in countries that do not subsidize their farmers, such abuse of power by the privileged corporations often leaves the farmers impoverished and destitute. For example, the coffee growers in Asia and Central America cannot afford to buy a cup of their own coffee at the famous brand urban coffee shops in their own countries.[6]

---

[6]Raj Patel, *Stuffed & Starved: The Hidden Battle for the World Food System* (Great Britain: Portobello 2007. Brooklyn: Melville, 2008). Print.

Countless individual farmers are going out of business world-wide. The highest suicide rate throughout the world is amongst farmers. Since the late 1990s, over 25,000 farmers have committed suicide in India alone.[7,8] This may not have an impact on the minds of people sitting in far away places enjoying their pre-packaged dinners. But imagine the impact on the families of the framers, and how much arable land must be lying unused as a result of the suicides. Can the world, or more important, a country like India afford this catastrophic trend? Can world hunger be really eliminated if this trend continues?

Deforestation is another manifestation of the reckless and insensitive behavior of the powerful and privileged human race.[9] In the late 1800s, industrialization led to the clearing of almost half the world's forests. According to a 2005 report by the United Nations' (UN) Food and Agriculture Organization (FAO), the earth's total forest area decreases by 13 million hectares per year.

---

[7]"Monsanto." *Wikipedia, The Free Encyclopedia.* Wikipedia, The Free Encyclopedia, 15 July 2010. Web. 15 July 2010.
http://en.wikipedia.org/wiki/Monsanto

[8] "Farmers' Suicides in India." *Wikipedia, The Free Encyclopedia.* Wikipedia, The Free Encyclopedia, 7 July 2010. Web. 15 July 2010.
http://en.wikipedia.org/wiki/Farmerspercent27_suicides_in_India

[9]"Deforestation." *Wikipedia, The Free Encyclopedia.* Wikipedia, The Free Encyclopedia, 15 July 2010. Web. 15 July 2010.
http://en.wikipedia.org/wiki/Deforestation

Below are the major causes of deforestation:

◊ Subsistence farming

◊ Commercial agriculture

◊ Large-scale cattle ranching

◊ Logging

◊ Fuel wood usage

◊ Extractive industry

◊ Industrial pollution

Most of these practices have short-term economic gains. But, in the long run they result in loss of income and often permanent deterioration of the ecosystem.

Survival of the Fittest and Acts of Brutality

Some people consider life to be survival of the fittest and go about their lives as though nothing were wrong. But, what if there were another, more superior, species on the planet or there were visiting extraterrestrials better endowed, more intelligent and more creative than humans? And what if they conducted their worldly business with ruthless disregard for plant and animal life on the planet. And what if they emulated human behavior toward other life forms? Consider the horrific possibilities. What if they captured humans, kept them bound in cramped quarters, and raised them on farms to serve as a source of food; neutered the cute little ones and kept them in cages as household pets. Whisked away babies as delicacies for the discerning palates or dropped alive into boiling oil or water to preserve the softness of their flesh. Stole milk from nursing mothers and fed it to their own young ones. Used human skin for upholstery—the soft skin of babies used by the privileged few. Periodically plucked human hair and used it as yarn—long, black shiny hair being reserved for special occasions. Amputated their fingers and toes for esthetics and hygiene. Chained large and ferocious men for use as guards, the rare and unusual kept along with other exotic animals in zoos, the agile reserved for entertainment in circuses, the strong for toiling on agribusiness farms or for transportation, the fierce and aggressive ones for fighting either in wars or in bull rings before large crowds for entertainment and the weak as bait to trap other species. Some sacrificed at sacred altars to appease their gods. Hunted humans living in the wild for sport; wore their teeth and cartilages as jewelry; taxidermists prepared human bodies and body parts to be displayed on walls. Ordered mass culling for overpopulation of human beings or upon the threat of an epidemic such as mad human disease or a flu pandemic and buried their bodies in mass graves.

These acts of brutality would be instantly labeled cruel and inhumane. Yet, humans go about their lives totally oblivious of such brutality toward most other life forms on the planet.

Yet, survival of the fittest seems to be the prevailing philosophy. Perhaps such ruthless insensitivity arises because some of them truly believe they are created in the image of God and thus bestowed with the Divine Power and Privilege. Others may even believe that they are reaping the rewards for good behavior in the past. Do such beliefs give them the absolute freedom to do exactly as they please? Have such people become desensitized and have they developed emotional blind spots?

How many stop and think of the plant and animal life lost every time they eat? How many think of the sacrifices made by other living creatures, including humans, when they consume anything? Some probably don't even give it a passing thought as long as it is convenient, suits their fancy and the price is right.

Fortunately, organizations such as PETA do care and appeal for compassion. They devote their meager resources to promote the humane treatment of animals.

The video posted on the website of People for the Ethical Treatment of Animals (PETA)[10] is one example of human brutality: http://www.peta.org/feat/ChineseFurFarms/index.asp. It shows how animals are skinned alive for their fur, and left to die thereafter. One can only imagine the agonizing pain these helpless animals suffer during and after the entire process.

Thanks also to the efforts of the United Nations (UN), along with other organizations such as Community Forestry International, Cool Earth, The Nature Conservancy, World Wide Fund for Nature, Conservation International, African Conservation Foundation and Greenpeace, the world's forests have a chance of surviving human onslaught. Some of the programs offer monetary or other incentives to countries to limit deforestation, encourage reforestation and use cyclic agriculture that replenishes soil nutrients.

---

[10]"Animals Used for Clothing." *PETA*. People for the Ethical Treatment of Animals, 2010. Web. 15 July 2010.
http://www.peta.org/actioncenter/clothing.asp

With growing awareness in the world, one can only hope that all creation will eventually be treated with respect because, despite modern discoveries and medical advancements, humans remain mortals just like the others.

Let's pray that the human race never escapes from Earth to spread its iniquity elsewhere.

— C. S. Lewis (1898–1963) British medievalist and author

If the whole human race lay in one grave, the epitaph on its headstone might well be: "It seemed a good idea at the time."

— Rebecca West (1892–1983) British novelist and critic

Chapter 2
Power and Privilege in the Family

God could not be everywhere; therefore, he made mothers.

– A Jewish saying

There is an angel in the family who, by the mysterious influence of grace, of sweetness, and of love, renders the fulfillment of duties less wearisome, sorrows less bitter.

– Giuseppe Mazzini (1805–1872) Italian philosopher

The family with an old person in it possesses a jewel.

– A Chinese saying

The word "family" conjures up feelings of harmony, trust and nurturing. It is the quintessential functioning unit of modern society, in which the young and able-bodied members take care of the infants and children, as well as the weak and old. Yet, the concordance seems superficial. Scratch the surface and a host of hierarchies with their attendant privileges and power, dictated by culture and tradition, become apparent.

Male Preference

In some cultures, males in the family enjoy a privileged status. The birth of a boy is celebrated with festivities, while that of a girl is mourned. The well-being and future happiness of some of these families seemingly depends on the birth of sons. The strangest part of such a practice is that females in the family, including the mothers, are willing participants in a system that empowers the sons from birth and later grants them a privileged status in society. The family wealth and attention is showered on the boys from day one. They enjoy the best food, the best accommodations, the best clothes, the best education, and the best mode of conveyance, among other privileges. The daughters in the family simply watch enviously or attend to family chores.

In the male-preferential cultures, the elders often bless their younger family members with the statement, "May you be blessed with sons." On the surface, this seems benign, but it is fraught with gender bias. Such biased phrases and expressions abound. For example, in most Indian languages there are separate words for daughter and son, e.g., in Hindi, *beti* and *beta,* respectively. It is customary for the family elders, including the women, to address their favorite daughters as male, i.e., *beta,* instead of *beti.* In other words, one often hears them say to their daughters: "Thank you, *beta,*" or "God bless you, *beta.*" The elders, by so doing, are elevating the status of the daughter to that of a son. Most girls (even grown women) feel honored to be so lovingly blessed or elevated. The practice is so pervasive, that, almost universally, nobody notices that it is loaded with centuries of gender bias.

In such cultures, sons are preferred over daughters even today. This becomes apparent when one examines the utilization of medical ultrasounds routinely to prenatally determine the sex of the unborn fetus so that the undesirable females can be aborted. The statistics of female abortions are shocking.[11] According to the data presented on the website, Gendercide.org, in Mumbai (formerly Bombay), India, 7,999 out of 8,000 of the aborted fetuses were females. And, if for some reason the female fetus is not aborted, then after birth, the mother may either willingly or under coercion abandon or give up for adoption the newborn girl. The object there is to raise only sons. Consider this global problem:

◊ *Killed, aborted or neglected, at least 100 million girls have disappeared—and the number is rising.*

　　　　　　　　　　– In Gendercide, *The Economist,* 4 March 2010.

Today, in modern India, despite the 1994 Prohibition of Sex Selection Act, and the 2002 law against such selective abortions, medical sonography is used extensively to determine the gender of a fetus, and, if found to be female, she is aborted. It is estimated that in some parts of the country, four out of five female fetuses are aborted.

What will be the long-term effects of such practices? Will it result in a disproportionately high male to female ratio in the population? Will such an imbalance create a more aggressive male-dominated society where women will be more subjugated? Could this lead to more territorial wars and genocidal rapes?

---

[11]Indu Grewal and J. Kishore, "Female Foeticide in India." *IHEU.* International Humanist and Ethical Union, 1 May 2004. Web. 16 July 2010. http://www.iheu.org/female-foeticide-in-india

Could women become endangered in some parts of the world? Or will the pendulum swing in favor of the few remaining girls so that they get preferential treatment in society? Will the young ladies start demanding a hefty price from prospective grooms? Time alone will tell.

Preference for sons exists despite the fact that educated and financially independent daughters are increasingly taking on the responsibility of caring for the elders of the family.[12] Perhaps all those who participate in the unfair practices that eliminate females ought to think long and hard about the eventuality of their old age. Their unwanted daughters may be their only caregivers. And it may be wise not to say to these daughters, "You are just like a son." Hopefully, the younger generation of women will be more accepting of daughters and not buckle under pressure from family elders to bear and raise only sons.

In some families, women who give birth to sons are treated with greater respect. Marriages are conveniently annulled, wives divorced, or even killed, if they do not bear at least one male heir. A notable example in history is that of Henry VIII, King of England (1491–1547), who had six wives. He considered Jane Seymour, his third wife, to be his only "true" wife because only she had given him a male heir.

---

[12]"Daughters as Care Giver to Aged Parents." *Silver Innings: Blog for Senior Citizens*. 6 Mar. 2010. Web. 15 July 2010.
http://silverinnings.blogspot.com/2010/03/daughters-as-care-giver-to-aged-parents.html

This tradition of having male heirs is called "male primogeniture." It gives the first-born male child, or the only male child, greater status than other family members. This special privilege gives the first-born male child the right to inherit the entire estate, to the exclusion of all other siblings, including older sisters.[13]

Male primogeniture is still practiced in many countries of the modern world today. An "heir apparent" is almost always a male who cannot be displaced from inheriting the family wealth. A daughter may inherit, but only by default. In other words, a daughter ranks behind all her brothers, regardless of age. In contrast, an "heir presumptive" is the term for a conditional heir, usually a female, who is temporarily in line to inherit, only to be displaced if a son is subsequently born in the family. Her Royal Highness (HRH) Queen Elizabeth II (born in 1926) of the United Kingdom (UK) was one such heir presumptive during the reign of her father, King George VI (1895̄1952), because he could have fathered a legitimate son any time before dying. Even today, these terms are commonly used by royal families; they give their heirs apparent the generic title of Crown Prince, or a more specific title, such as Prince of Orange in the Netherlands, or Prince of Wales in the UK.

Recently, there has been an introduction of *absolute* primogeniture. According to this new concept, a female heir apparent is now possible. In recent times, a few European royal families

[13]"Primogeniture."*Wikipedia, The Free Encyclopedia.* Wikipedia, The Free Encyclopedia, 8 July 2010. Web. 15 July 2010.
http://en.wikipedia.org/wiki/Primogeniture

have adopted (or have been forced by their democratic popular governments to adopt) such a system. Currently, worldwide, there is only one female heir apparent: HRH the Crown Princess Victoria of Sweden.[14] Interestingly, she was not heir apparent at the time of her birth in 1977, but was given the status only in 1980, following a change in the Swedish Act of Succession. Until then, her younger brother, Carl Philip, who was two years younger, was heir apparent for a few months until the passage of the Act.

There were 18 heirs apparent as of 2008, spread all across the globe from Japan to Canada.[15] And, yes, all except one were men. For a list of the heirs apparent, please see Appendix A.

The British parliament blocked attempts to revise the succession laws in the UK *even* in the Twenty-first Century. Furthermore, the UK, one of the leading modern democracies of the world—consisting of four countries: England, Northern Ireland, Scotland and Wales—interestingly, is always called *king*dom, even if there is a *queen* on the throne. It was not called United Queendom during Queen Victoria's reign, or even during the reign of the current HRH Queen Elizabeth II. Furthermore, the UK and the countries such as Canada, Australia, and New Zealand, all part of the Commonwealth Realms, share some common values and goals. These include the promotion

---

[14]"Victoria, Crown Princess of Sweden." *Wikipedia, The Free Encyclopedia.* Wikipedia, The Free Encyclopedia, 15 July 2010. Web. 15 July 2010. http://en.wikipedia.org/wiki/Victoria,_Crown_Princess_of_Sweden

[15]"Heir Apparent." *Wikipedia, The Free Encyclopedia.* Wikipedia, The Free Encyclopedia, 19 Jun. 2010. Web. 15 July 2010. http://en.wikipedia.org/wiki/Heir_apparent

of democracy, *human rights*, good governance, the rule of law, individual liberty, egalitarianism, free trade, multilateralism and world peace. Yet these modern democracies deny the basic human right of equality to the female members of their royal families and extend special privileges and powers only to their male heirs.

Marriage and Sex

In most modern societies, women are not privileged to have an identity of their own so it is customary for them to adopt the last names of their husbands after marriage. However, a growing number of professional women are keeping their maiden names. Nevertheless, at social occasions or when their names appear on printed invitations, these very independent professional women often get lumped together with their husbands, as Mr. and Mrs. so-and-so with the husband's last name on the invitation, and almost never the other way around. To make the system fair, hyphenated last names have made an appearance on the matrimonial horizon. The married woman keeps her maiden name and adopts the husband's last name with a hyphen in between. The children raised in such families also inherit the hyphenated last names. In some Spanish-speaking countries, a woman keeps her maiden last name, and the children inherit their mother's last name. However, officially, the woman must add her husband's name as well, connected with *de,* translated "of," as in "belonging to." However, regardless of how the last names are assigned, the practice perpetuates the use of patriarchal last names.[16] The matriarch remains obscure.

---

[16]Jeanette F. Chaplin. Personal communication. 25 June 2010.

In some male-dominated cultures, domestic privileges of the groom do not end with simply choosing a wife to live with happily ever after. In fact, marriage is only the beginning of lifelong privileges. From the outset, wives are dehumanized and treated like chattel. The young brides are even given a new first name based on the whim and fancy of the groom or his family. For example, Vimla is called Asha after marriage. Furthermore, they are expected to wait hand and foot, not only on the groom but also the entire family; work tirelessly every single moment from dawn to dusk; and last, but not least, serve as a sex slave to the husband and provide the services on demand. If the services extended by the wife are not to the full satisfaction of the husband or his family, she can be discarded for a new (and often younger) wife. Wives, on the other hand, do not often have any option. Such abusive practices are largely legitimized and perpetuated by systematically camouflaging them under the banner of culture, tradition and religion—often all male-dominated.

In polygamous religions, there is a growing trend whereby the aging men of the family enjoy the privilege of acquiring a multitude of ever-younger brides. The practice resembles a male-dominated cult of sex maniacs swapping their young daughters, often as young as nine years—all in the name of a God-given privilege and family values. The concept of family under such circumstances resembles legalized rape and prostitution.

In certain parts of the world, the privilege of selecting a marriage partner rests solely with the eligible men. Often the women being considered for the matrimonial relationship have no say in the selection process. The arrangement is further complicated by the tradition of the dowry, whereby the girl's family is obligated to give the newlyweds, and sometimes the groom's family, cash, a house, a car, gold, jewelry, home appliances and other material things at the time of marriage. The concept of the dowry was originally designed to help the newlyweds start a new life together. But, over time, the practice has turned into a business transaction. There is intense negotiating similar in nature to the kind encountered for the purchase of real estate or automobiles. The price tag of the dowry is determined by the looks and educational qualifications of the groom. Better-looking and more educated grooms have a higher price tag. One would think that education would steer the grooms away from this unfair practice. But that is generally not the case. As a result, dowry giving has become so burdensome to the bride's family that it is often left impoverished after marrying a daughter. Some daughters never get married as a result. And if the bride's family cannot deliver on the promised dowry, the bride is burnt alive. Little wonder that sons, and not daughters, are preferred. Fortunately, there are increasing number of educated people, albeit a minority, who are equally accepting of their daughters and grooms who do not demand a dowry.

If marriage has been reduced to a business transaction and price tags of dowry negotiated by the family (male) elders, then perhaps it may be worthwhile to involve the bride-to-be in the negotiations. What would that achieve? First, the bride would have a say in the selection of the groom. Second, she could add on the charges for her labor as a domestic worker, not only for the work expected after marriage, but also for work done since early childhood while growing up in her biological family. If these "undesirable daughters" and "financial burdens" were paid minimum wages for their domestic work, the giving of a dowry at the time of marriage would only be fair—as these young girls usually perform an astronomical number of hours of domestic work starting in childhood. Alimony after divorce should also factor in the hours of domestic work performed during the marriage. If girls and women were paid for their work, there would be millions of female millionaires, and perhaps Africa would have the highest Gross Domestic Product (GDP) in the world.

In some cultures, families expect their female members to be covered from head-to-toe in a veil if they step outside the home. It is considered immoral to leave home without them. Women without the veils are considered evil temptresses and risk being attacked. Meanwhile, men move about in society unrestricted, even though they are the perpetrators of violence, especially sexual violence, against women.

Violence against women is not limited to certain cultures. In fact, it is a global problem. The following statements were released in 2007 by the UN and its subsidiary, the United Nations Development Fund for women (UNIFEM):

◊ *Violence against women and girls continues unabated in every continent, country and culture. . . . Too often, it is covered up or tacitly condoned.* – UN Secretary-General Ban Ki-Moon, 8 Mar. 2007

◊ *Violence against women and girls is a problem of pandemic proportions. At least one out of every three women around the world has been beaten, coerced into*

sex, or otherwise abused in her lifetime—with the
abuser usually someone in the family – UNIFEM

◊ *The costs of [family] partner violence in the United States*
alone exceed US$5.8 billion per year – UNIFEM

According to data from the General Accounting Office in the U.S. and a 1997 report by the FBI reveals some discouraging facts:[17, 18, 19]

◊ *Nearly one in every four women is beaten or raped by*
a partner

◊ *Three women are killed by a current or former intimate*
partner each day

◊ *15 percent of sexual assaults and rape victims are under*
the age of 12; 29 percent are aged 12–17

◊ *93 percent of juvenile sexual assault victims know their*
attackers; 34 percent of the attackers are family members

◊ *Every year, approximately 1.3 million women are physi-*
cally assaulted by an intimate partner

Such treatment of women in the family throughout history has always had this sinister aspect glossed over by the male-dominated societies. Furthermore, despite the looming presence

---

[17]Dean G. Kilpatrick, "Rape and Sexual Assault." *MUSC*. Medical University of South Carolina, 2000. Web. 15 July 2010.
http://www.musc.edu/vawprevention/research/sa.shtml

[18]Rape, Abuse and Incest National Network. Web. 21 July 2010
http://www.rainn.org/get-information/statistics/sexual-assault-victims

[19]Domestic Violence and Sexual Assault Fact sheet. Web 21 July 2010 .
http://www.nnedv.org/docs/Stats/NNEDV_DVSA_factsheet2010

of religious and common laws, there is a booming trade globally by which young girls and women are forced into prostitution. It is such a lucrative business that organized criminals from the East to the West have operations all over the world:

◊   *An estimated 600,000 women and girls are trafficked across international borders each year*

◊   *Between 27 million to 200 million people are living as sex slaves*[20]

To get a glimpse of the shocking details of brutality towards women, one can read the national bestseller, *Half the Sky*, co-authored by Nicholas D. Kristoff and Sheryl WuDunn.[21] The book also offers a list of charitable organizations that help women escape sexual slavery and become financially independent. Some of the organizations are listed in Appendix B.

Just imagine what an unfair and cruel world it would be if females were the privileged and powerful members in the family and treated males as men have treated women throughout the centuries. Imagine if male fetuses were systematically aborted, drastically reducing the male population on the planet. What if the birth of boys was mourned, while that of girls celebrated, and if the girls got the best of everything, including a university education while the boys watched in envy? And the women elders in the family punished the wayward "evil" eyes of young men so that they would not get aroused at the sight of young girls, but learned to be virtuous and

---

[20]Trafficking in Persons Report June 2005 U.S. State Dep't, 2005 Web. 20 July 2010. http://www.state.gov/documents/organization/47255.pdf..

[21]Nicholas D. Kristoff and Sheryl WuDunn, *Half the Sky*. (New York Vintage Books, 2010). Print.

chivalrous instead? Or women of the family kept their boys from getting an education so that they could grow up to be docile and subservient husbands to their wives and thereby bring honor to the family? What if any behavior by young men bringing dishonor to the family resulted in severe punishment, including genital mutilation and honor killing? What if women got to pick their husbands, and if one did not suit their needs, got another, and yet another—each one younger, more able-bodied, and more handsome? Then the women kept the multitude of husbands housebound and used them as domestic and sex slaves.

How deplorable life would be for men. It would be most unfair to treat them in such a fashion. And yet, too many women around the world are subjected to such treatment, all in the name of family values, tradition and honor.

Why female members of the family have done nothing over the millennia to change the plight of their lot will remain a mystery. Perhaps women in the patriarchal, male-dominated, cultures developed large emotional blind spots. Maybe they feared for their lives; perhaps they still do.

Women also abuse their status in the family. Some women elders verbally and physically abuse their daughters-in-law. In addition, a pecking order usually exists whereby the female elders make all the decisions. Fortunately, such privileges do not extend beyond the mundane day-to-day operations of the household, such as planning the day's menu, cooking, cleaning and doing laundry.

Self-inquiring and educated young women of modern civilization could receive some inspiration from the matrilineal cultures. They existed in ancient Egypt; in parts of Western Sumatra,

Indonesia; in the states of Kerala, Karnataka, Tamil Nadu and Meghalaya, India; among the Nakhi and the Mosuo of China; among the Basque people in Spain; in the Hopi, Navajo, Cherokee and Gitksan Native American tribes; in the Akan of Ghana, the Berber in north and west Africa; and, last, but not least, among the Jews.[22]

Most societies have clearly spelled out laws on the institution of marriage. And the common laws pertaining to marriage are invariably influenced by the dominant religion. The most prevalent custom worldwide is a monogamous arrangement of fidelity between a husband and his wife. But how sacrosanct is this arrangement? It is rather sad that family members, including the elders, and religious leaders have throughout history ignored the huge differences between the written laws and their actual practice. Men consider their sexual gratification as a right in most societies, regardless of religious beliefs or marital status. According to a study published by Shere Hite, 72 percent of married men in modern Western society have extramarital sex.[23] The explanation given for such male behavior is "instinctive male sex drive." There may even be a prevailing sense among men that "all real men do it" for recreation. In contrast, such recreation for women is fraught with dangers—especially the danger of an unwanted pregnancy. And it is often the woman's responsibility to cope

[22]"Matrilineality." *Wikipedia, The Free Encyclopedia*. Wikipedia, The Free Encyclopedia, 4 July 2010. Web. 15 July 2010.
http://en.wikipedia.org/wiki/Matrilineality#Matrilineal_surname.

[23]Shere Hite, *Women as Revolutionary Agents of Change - The Hite Reports: Sexuality, Love, & Emotion* (London: Bloomsbury, 1993. London: Sceptre-Hodder & Stoughton, 1994). Print.

with such consequences—*even* though it takes a man to willingly partake in the act.

There are many news reports of what a pervasive problem teenage pregnancy has become in modern society.[24, 25] But do all well-meaning parents keep a watchful eye on the behavior of their teenage boys as closely as that of their daughters? Are teenage girls more privileged in this regard? Could parents really care more for their daughters? Of course not! The parents simply do not want to deal with unwanted teenage pregnancies. Why do parents fail to see that the behavior of the teenage boys is half the problem? By allowing their teenage boys more freedom, aren't the parents endangering the daughters of their neighbors? Is this lack of understanding of the entire scenario because of indoctrination or emotional blind spots toward this problem? Or is it simply because men are in charge of maintaining order at home, as well as in society? And if most men really believe that all "real men do it," then can there really be a fair solution to *all* unwanted pregnancies, not just teenage pregnancies?

In most instances, women shoulder the burden of unwanted pregnancies. How often does one see graphic pictures of malnourished infants and children clinging to their mothers

---

[24]Robin Elise Weiss, "Teen Pregnancy." *About*. About.com, 2010. Web. 15 July 2010.
http://pregnancy.about.com/cs/teenpregnancy/a/teenpreg.htm;

[25]Daniel J. DeNoon, "Teen Pregnancy Surges." *WebMD*. WebMD, 26 Jan. 2010. Web. 15 July 2010.
http://www.webmd.com/parenting/news/20100126/teen-pregnancy-surges

from drought-affected or war-torn regions of the world? These mothers often have little to keep their own body and soul together. Are these mothers simply irresponsible? It does not take much to assign blame on the women. But to get the real answer, one would have to ask: Were the women driven by desperation or coerced by a selfish and irresponsible male member of the community, including their husbands?

Is society's disregard for irresponsible male behavior and the prevalence of recreational sex eventually going to make the concept of marriage obsolete? Time will tell. But in the mean time, as long as men in male-dominated societies cannot take 'NO' for an answer and recreational sex is the norm, it would be better for society to give women full reproductive rights. The dominant religions opposed to birth control ought to reconsider their dogma. Wouldn't the world be a much better place for everyone if all children were born to willing and healthy mothers, who could afford to raise their children in a safe and nurturing homes—with due help from the fathers?

One major problem arising from irresponsible male behavior is the global spread of HIV and AIDS. Married women are powerless to keep from contracting HIV from their husbands due to their blatantly lecherous escapades. In countries such as India, wives dare not even suggest the use of condoms, even if it means protecting the unborn baby during pregnancy. Suggesting the use of condoms would only result in physical violence and coerced sex. Furthermore, the wives are so fearful of being abandoned by their husbands and family, they choose not to ever be tested or treated for HIV.[26]

---

[26]Anjali Gandhi, ed. *Women's Work, Health and Empowerment* (New Delhi: Aakar, 2006). Print.

Can the global pandemic be controlled in the face of such abuse of power by married men? One can only imagine the frustration of healthcare workers who are trying to prevent the spread of HIV and AIDS.

Are men the only ones to blame for the ills in society? No. Women too abuse their status as females. The commonest way women do so is by flaunting their sexuality to tease and attract male attention by the way they dress and conduct themselves. The implicit messages they broadcast say, "Look, but do not touch." Even in the most advanced Westernized societies such messages are often misinterpreted by the men as tacit invitations. Then the women turn around and accuse men of assault, sending them to serve jail sentences. But such cases are few and far between.

Adultcentrism

Adultcentrism is a new term in family therapy to describe the tendency of adults to view the world only from an adult perspective and, in so doing, not understand or appreciate how children and young people, or even the elderly, view things.[27] Children are considered "incomplete," "incompetent," and meant to

---

[27]"Adultcentrism." *Wikipedia, The Free Encyclopedia.* Wikipedia, The Free Encyclopedia, 21 Mar. 2010. Web. 15 July 2010. http://en.wikipedia.org/wiki/Adultcentrism.

"exercise authority" on.[28, 29] The elderly are viewed as a burden. Such a mindset empowers the adults to treat children and elders unfairly.

The naming of a newborn in the family is one of the most benign forms of the all-pervasive adultcentrism. The event is often a special occasion, celebrated by the adults. Do adults ever consider allowing their children to choose their first names? How many children grow up hating the first names assigned to them by adults of the family? With the advent of birth certificates, the newborn not only gets the first name, but also inherits the family's last name, which is almost always patriarchal. Fortunately, in the U.S, people can and sometimes do change their names.

There is an unusual patrilineal system in practice in Iceland based on the Old Norse method whereby the individual's last name is the father's (not the mother's) first name with a sex-specific suffix such as -sson or -sonur for a son and -dattir or -dottir for a daughter (e.g., Hermansson or Hermandattir). So, individual identity in Iceland rests strictly with first names, which are used even on formal occasions.[30] But even in this system, the

---

[28]Christopher G. Petr, "Adultcentrism in Practice With Children." Families in Society: The Journal of Contemporary Human Services. Families International Inc. 1992. Print.

[29]"Ruth Benedict." *Wikipedia, The Free Encyclopedia*. Wikipedia, The Free Encyclopedia, 11 July 2010. Web. 15 July 2010. http://en. wikipedia.org/wiki/Ruth_Benedict#Patterns_of_Culture Benedict 1934

[30]"Icelandic Surnames." *Gaming Geeks*. Gaming Geeks, n.d. Web. 15 July 2010. http://www.gaminggeeks.org/Resources/KateMonk/Europe-Scandinavia/Iceland/Surnames.htm

mothers' names remain elusive in the male-dominated patriarchal system. Consider these examples of patriarchal Gaelic last names from Ireland: O'Neal, O'Brien, McDonald, and McCain. One never sees O'Nancy, O'Barbara, McDonna, or McCatherine.

An ugly extension of adultcentrism is that of child laundering, very similar to money laundering. Children are often kidnapped or taken away from their biological families—against their will—and sold as orphans to unsuspecting adopting families.[31] Some adoption agencies may even be involved in such child-laundering rackets. Fortunately, most adoptive parents provide a loving home environment to these children. But, could some adopted children end up as domestic or sex slaves? What safeguards does society have to protect these adopted children? Would it not be wise to institute follow-up procedures to ensure that they are not being abused in any way?

Adultcentrism also results in the abuse of the elderly. The power-wielding able-bodied young adult family members subject the elders to neglect, and verbal and physical abuse as they begin to fail physically and mentally. A significant number of the aged get sent to elder care centers against their will, where perhaps the abuse is worse.

---

[31]"Child Laundering." *Wikipedia, The Free Encyclopedia.* Wikipedia, The Free Encyclopedia, 19 Apr. 2010. Web. 15 July 2010. http://en.wikipedia.org/wiki/Child_laundering

About half a million adults aged 60 and over are abused or neglected in domestic settings in the U.S.[32] The elderly have their money and valuables stolen by their own family members. The percentage of such cases that come to the attention of the authorities is low. In the US. alone, current estimates put the overall reporting of financial exploitation of the elders at approximately 1 in 25. In other words, there may be at least 5 million "financially-abused" elderly victims each year.[33]

❑ ❑ ❑

Over the millennia, society has strived to preserve the family unit, and for good reasons. Life without the family would be fraught with hardship and peril. Would it not serve humanity much more if children were raised in loving environments to be caring, confident and mindful human beings?[34] Why isn't every member of the family treated with love and respect and allowed to play an active role? The collective wisdom of all members of the family—young and old, male and female—could only enhance the quality of life both at home and beyond, and the whole world would enjoy greater harmony.

---

[32]The National Center on Elder Abuse at the American Public Human Services Association in Collaboration with Westat, Sept. 1998, *The National Elder Abuse Incidence Study* (1998). Web. 20 July 2010. http://www.aoa.gov/AoARoot/AoA_Programs/Elder_Rights/Elder_Abuse/docs/ABuseReport_Full.pdf

[33]John F. Wasik, "The Fleecing of America's Elderly," *Consumers Digest* Mar./Apr. 2000. Print.

[34]Julianna Lyddon, *"Raising a Happy Spirit: The Inner Wisdom of Parenting."* USA, Minibuk 2010. Print.

We've begun to raise daughters more like sons, but few have the courage to raise our sons more like our daughters.

– Gloria Steinem

A daughter is a daughter for life; a son is a son until he finds a wife.

– Italian saying

Chapter 3
Power and Privilege in Academia

Academic institutions are places where access to power and influence is rationed.

– Glenn Cartman Loury (born in 1948)
Alumnus of MIT, Professor of the Social Sciences
and Professor of Economics at Brown University

[May] our wisdom grow with our power.

– Thomas Jefferson (1743–1826)
Third President of the United States and
principal author of
The Declaration of Independence (1776)

Conventional wisdom suggests that time spent on education at good academic institutions is one of the best lifetime investments for people who wish to be successful. Whether one wishes to become an engineer, a physician, a lawyer or a career politician, the privileges of higher education at renowned institutions do not simply end with graduation ceremonies.

Stamp of Approval of the "Old Boys' Club"

Those who are privileged to obtain a university education at renowned institutions get a stamp of approval for a lifetime, regardless of their competence or individual performance; their acquisition and possession of real knowledge and wisdom often seem perfunctory. Furthermore, the best paying jobs of any industry go to graduates of such academic institutions. The doors to the highest offices in a nation also open more readily to those with degrees from such institutions. Today, the wealthy, the privileged and the powerful men in the world are products of such high-ranking institutions. These institutions are supporters of excellence, but they seem to be promoting the interests of the privileged few from all parts of the world. Some examples of academic institutions that "make" world leaders are the London School of Economics of the University of London, Oxford University and Harvard University, to name a few.

Among the alumni of London School of Economics (LSE) are 15 Nobel laureates, but it boasts 46 heads of states or governments, and monarchs, including leaders of countries such as Canada, India, Japan and the U.S. Many former and current Chief Executive Officers (CEOs) of multinationals are also alumni of the LSE.[35] For a list of LSE alumni who became heads of state, see Appendix C. The resignation, in early 2011, of the head of LSE for his alleged connections with the Gaddafi regime in Libya seems like the tip of an iceberg. [http://www.guardian.co.uk/education/2011/mar/03/lse-director-resigns-gaddafi-scandal]

---

[35]"List of London School of Economics People."*Wikipedia, The Free Encyclopedia*. Wikipedia, The Free Encyclopedia, 29 Jun. 2010. Web. 15 July 2010. http://en.wikipedia.org/wiki/ List_of_London_School_of_Economics_people

The alumni of Oxford are called Oxonians. There have been 46 Oxonian heads of state or governments worldwide, in countries such as Australia, Canada, India and the U.S.[36] Oxford has to its credit 25 prime Ministers in the UK alone. Oxonians have also become CEOs and Board members in companies all over the world. The power-wielding media magnate from Australia, Rupert Murdoch, is an Oxonian.[37] For a list of alumni of Oxford who became heads of state see Appendix D.

Although relatively new on the scene, across the Atlantic, Harvard University has 41 Nobel laureates, and 35 alumni who have been leaders of countries such as Canada, Greece and the U.S. In the U.S. alone, it boasts eight presidents and two vice presidents. Several dozen CEOs, board members, and chief financial officers (CFOs) in leading business organizations all over the world are Harvard graduates, including the current chairman of the Federal Reserve, Mr. Ben Bernanke.[38,39] For a list of Harvard alumni who have become heads of state, please see Appendix E.

---

[36]"Oxford University," *Wikipedia, The Free Encyclopedia.* Wikipedia, The Free Encylopedia. 29 Nov. 2010. Web. 30 Nov 2010. http://en.wikipedia.org/wiki/University_of_Oxford

[37]"List of University of Oxford People in Public Life Overseas." *Wikipedia, The Free Encyclopedia.* Wikipedia, The Free Encyclopedia, 3 July 2010. Web. 15 July 2010. http://en.wikipedia.org/wiki/List_of_University_of_Oxford_people_in_public_life_overseas

[38]"List of Harvard University People." *Wikipedia, The Free Encyclopedia.* Wikipedia, The Free Encyclopedia, 13 July 2010. Web. 15 July 2010. http://en.wikipedia.org/wiki/List_of_Harvard_University_people

[39]"Ben Bernanke." *Wikipedia, The Free Encyclopedia.* Wikipedia, The Free Encyclopedia, 25 Sep. 2010. Web. 29 Sep. 2010. http://en.wikipedia.org/wiki/Ben_Bernanke

One hopes that access to these august institutions is predominantly based on merit, innate intelligence, and qualifying entrance examination scores. But, is it remotely possible that a significant number of world leaders from such institutions could have been admitted because of their privileged backgrounds? And, if so, what purpose do such "back door" admissions of undeserving students from privileged families serve? Do they serve a short-term financial gain? In other words, are hefty donations sought from the guardians of such students, who are often wealthy and powerful? Or does such a practice serve the long-term geopolitical goals in the world to promote modern secular democracy and the free market economy? Do such individuals truly acquire leadership skills at these renowned institutions? Or is it merely a global extension of the "Old Boys' Club?" Does the system seem to allow men, who already enjoy a privileged status in society, to remain privileged for generations thereafter, often wielding considerable social and political power all over the world.

The former Soviet Union had an "Old Boys' Club" too. Although not strictly in an academic setting, the so-called *Nomenklatura* served a similar purpose.[40] Members of the *Nomenklatura* were considered the elites of the society who enjoyed special privileges and powers that average citizens did not. Among those perks were shopping at special stores with access to foreign merchandise; preference in obtaining housing, including the right to own a second home; access to holiday resorts; foreign travel;

---

[40]"Nomenklatura." *Wikipedia, The Free Encyclopedia*. Wikipedia, The Free Encyclopedia, 27 Jun. 2010. Web. 15 July 2010. http://en.wikipedia.org/wiki/Nomenklatura

higher education for their children at prestigious universities; and obtaining prestigious jobs. Literally, *Nomenklatura* was a list of names of distinguished Communist Party leaders. There were two separate lists: one of individuals appointed to key positions in the Soviet system and a second list of potential candidates for future appointments. Within the first list were members of the powerful *Politburo*, who held Ministerial and ambassadorial positions. The appointees in the Soviet system were forever beholden to their appointers, much like the vassals of the feudal system. Did such cronyism result in the ultimate failure of the Soviet system where mediocrity thrived?

Admissions Policy

In the scholarly book, *The Chosen: The Hidden History of Admission and Exclusion at Harvard, Yale, and Princeton* (New York: Houghton Mifflin, 2005), Jerome Karabel, Professor of Sociology at the University of California, Berkeley and Co-director of the Berkeley Project on Equal Opportunity, laid bare the manipulation of admissions policies at these three academic institutions. In the early 1900s, the Big Three (Harvard, Yale, and Princeton universities) changed their admissions policies from a merit-based system to one that took into consideration the ethnic background of applicants. The policy was changed to control the composition of the new admissions. At the time, this was primarily done by the dominant white Anglo-Saxon administrators to exclude the Jews and other immigrants, mostly from Eastern Europe. In other words, they admitted the less deserving Anglo-Saxon wards of wealthy donors or the politically-connected families. What purpose did this serve? Did it serve merit and excellence in education, or did it create an unfair practice that excluded the deserving Jewish and Catholic students from ever reaching their full potential?

After the lifting of restrictive quotas of immigration by the passage of the 1965 Immigration Act, there was a surge of Asian immigrants to the U.S. Within 20 years, the Asian population more than tripled from 1 million to 3.6 million. Like the Jews, the Asian Americans tended to have above average grades. But the admissions policies of universities were unfair to the children of these newer immigrants. The playing field at the top universities was perhaps a bit altered since the early 1900s, and the umpires different, but the new admissions policy used "discretion" by the new gatekeepers, and, as before, lacked transparency.[41] Emphasis was laid on intangible factors such as character and job experience, and not just merit. Obviously, the system was wide open to abuse by a select few in the organizations. These universities were setting "informal ceilings" on them by subjecting them to higher entry requirements. Not surprisingly, in the mid 1980s, the top universities were accused of discrimination against the Asian Americans.[42] After the involvement of the Office of Civil Rights (OCR) and the Department of Education and a thorough investigation, two members of Congress submitted a resolution to the House of Representatives urging universities to review their admissions policies.

---

[41]Jerome Karabe, *The Chosen: The Hidden History of Admissions and Exclusion at Harvard, Yale and Princeton* (New York: Houghton Mifflin Company. 2005). Print.

[42]William B. Reynolds (Assistant Attorney General), *Discrimination Against Asian-Americans In Higher Education: Evidence, Causes, and Cures.* Department of Justice, Washington DC Civil Rights Division Nov. 1988. Web. 20 July 2010. http://www.eric.ed.gov/PDFS/ED308730.pdf

Is the system likely to become fair? Over time, the old elites are likely to be replaced by new ones, with the rules changed to favor the dominant ethnic groups, who create their own definitions of "merit." The process, therefore, perpetuates elitism of a different flavor.

Another way by which privileged classes in the United States perpetuated unfairness in the college admissions process was the policy of early and binding admissions. This policy favored wealthy privileged applicants, who did not have to wait to see if they qualified for scholarships or other financial aid packages. It left the less fortunate, but truly deserving students, at a disadvantage. The practice is still prevalent in some colleges. Does this suggest an implicit quota system for the privileged? Who do the powerful decision makers promote? Could they be inadvertently promoting mediocrity by such early admissions? Where do the truly bright students—natural-born citizens go if they are denied the privilege of a higher education in their own country? Could this lead to brain drain?

A few decades ago, women and minority applicants were not generally able to get a higher education at some American universities. Pursuing higher education at these esteemed institutions was the privilege of only white men. For example, Princeton University began to admit women only in 1969. In 1974, the number of females admitted was 650, out of several thousand students admitted.[43] Today, finally, women enrolled

[43]"Princeton University." *Wikipedia, The Free Encyclopedia*. Wikipedia, The Free Encyclopedia, 12 July 2010. Web. 15 July 2010.
http://en.wikipedia.org/wiki/Princeton_University

in Princeton are equally privileged to get a higher education at the prestigious institution. In 2006, Princeton also announced its intention of terminating its early admissions policy, starting in 2012. There can now be hope for some real fairness in access to higher education.

Across the Atlantic, at Oxford University, the situation is no better. Despite the University's claims that its admissions policies avoid bias against candidates of certain socioeconomic or educational backgrounds, the fairness of Oxford admissions has remained inequitable. Even today, its admissions favor the privileged from private schools, with only a few selected from state schools. Such an elitist admissions policy remains a national controversy. As recently as 2000, Magdalen College at Oxford denied a deserving applicant because she came from a "working-class" background and a state school. This particular student became one of ten British students to win a £65,000 (~US $120,000) scholarship from Harvard University in the U.S. She graduated from Harvard in 2004, and finished her medical education in October 2008 from Wolfson College, Cambridge (UK); she graduated from medical school with honors. The exclusion on the basis of social class and regional prejudice rather than pure merit resulted in a political controversy in the UK.[44] A Labor party member of Parliament and former Prime Minister, Gordon Brown, accused Oxford of elitism and called its admissions policy a "disgrace."

---

[44]"Is Oxbridge Elitist?" Talking Point. *BBC News.* BBC, 31 May 2000. Web. 15 July 2010. http://news.bbc.co.uk/2/hi/talking_point/764767.stm

Women face other problems once they get admitted to universities. On co-ed college campuses, women have the added disadvantage of being exposed to greater risks of being assaulted or raped. There seems to be a subculture of fraternity practice that encourages "abusive sex." Most female students have little recourse, and the male-dominated institutions do not take meaningful disciplinary actions against the perpetrators.[45]

⬚ ⬚ ⬚

Attempts to make the academic institutions fair must address some questions. How does one define merit? Do children of the working poor, who are the victims of poor schooling have a fair representation in a meritocracy? Can different proverbial yardsticks be used to gauge merit, factoring in socioeconomic status? Should affirmative action remain in force? If so, then how can all deserving students get a fair chance in an over-crowded system? The answers may not be simple. But one fundamental aim of society must be to offer higher education to all students willing to achieve their highest potential. Perhaps distance learning over cyberspace may be a solution.

---

[45]Meryl Altman, "Acquaintance Rape on Campus: Policies and Pedagogies." *DePauw*. DePauw University, 3 Feb. 2005. Web. 15 July 2010. http://fs6. depauw.edu:50080/~scrary/Socialpercent20Justice/Merylpercent20 Altmanpercent20Acquaintancepercent20Rapepercent 20onpercent20 Campus.pdf

Academic careers

The staffing of academic institutions also appears to be a special privilege of a select few. Women and ethnic minorities such as blacks and Hispanics are not as privileged there either. Barriers to entry and advancement exist at two specific levels in their academic life. The first barrier is encountered early in their careers when they reach an imaginary threshold "beyond which gender [and race] no longer matters" and later as an impenetrable "glass ceiling" to advancement in their profession. At the first hurdle, women and minorities face difficulties advancing in any given field. However, the obstacles are removed once the male decision makers have seen enough evidence of their "worthiness," judged subjectively. At the second hurdle, women and minorities are simply denied top academic ranks and positions of authority.[46]

Figures released in 2007 by the American Association of Medical Schools are summarized in the table below.[47]

Academic rank	Percent males	Percent females
Instructor	7	7
Assistant professor	24	17
Associate Professor	15	6
Full Professor	20	4

[46]Henry Etzkowitz, et al, *Barriers to Women in Academic Science and Engineering.* 15 July 2010. Web. 20 July 2010. http://people.mills.edu/spertus/Gender/EKNU.html.

[47]"Women in U.S. Academic Medicine Statistics and Medical School Benchmarking, 2007-2008." *AAMC.* Association of American Medical Colleges, 1995-2010. Web. 15 July 2010. http://www.aamc.org/members/gwims/statistics/stats08/start.htm

From the table, it is obvious that women either remain tied to the lower academic ranks, leave for an alternative occupation or drop out of the work force entirely. For them, their gender becomes a hindrance to any promotion. Pregnancy is discouraged. Women faculty members who do become pregnant are encouraged to take leaves of absence without pay, which invariably results in permanent withdrawal from academic life. In Canada, there are almost 60 percent females in a medical school class, but only 30 percent pursue a career in medicine.[48] Do these women physicians face barriers to entry in the job market, or re-entry after pregnancies? Isn't this a colossal waste of talent and training while the sick deal with waiting lists? Even more unfair is that for women who forgo motherhood entirely, acceptance as equals in the academic world remains elusive.

This male-dominated hierarchy is fading, but ever so slowly. According to a report published in 2008 by the Association of American Medical Colleges, in 200203, 34 percent of all faculty were women, up from 30 percent; 12 percent of department chairs were women, up from 9 percent; and 10 percent of medical school deans were women, up from 8 percent.[49] These numbers say it all.

---

[48]Anita Palepu and Carol P. Herbert, "Medical Women in Academia: The Silences We Keep." *Can. Med. Assoc. J.*, Oct 2002; 167: 877 – 879. http://www.ncbi.nlm.nih.gov/pmc/articles/PMC128400/

[49]Jennifer Leadley et al, *Women in U.S. Academic Medicine. Statistics and Benchmarking Report: 2007-2008* (Washington, DC: AAMC, n.d.). 20 July 2010. http://www.aamc.org/members/gwims/statistics/stats08/ stats_report.pdf

Such gender-biased trends are prevalent not only in academic medicine but in every other field. Women across the board advance slowly, are tenured more slowly and earn less than men.[50]

The tables below illustrate the bleak progress women have made in academia during a five-year period:

Percentage of women faculty:

Academic Field	Percent in 2003	Percent in 1998
Business Schools	16	14
Engineering	10	10
Law	27	22
Medicine (clinical)	25	20

Percentage of tenured women faculty:

Academic Field	Percent in 2003	Percent in 1998
Business Schools	15	12
Engineering	7	6
Law	15	26
Medicine (clinical)	16	13

In 2001, the Ford Foundation sponsored a meeting to discuss the problem of under-representation of women in academia. A statement was approved by (mostly male) leaders of nine leading

---

[50]Virginia Valian, *Why So Slow: The Advancement of Women.* Web. 20 July 2010. http://mitworld.mit.edu/video/80/

academic institutions: the California Institute of Technology, University of California at Berkeley, Harvard University, University of Michigan, Massachusetts Institute of Technology, University of Pennsylvania, Princeton University, Stanford University and Yale University. Their leaders agreed to do the following:

◊ Analyze the salaries and the proportion of other university resources provided to women faculty

◊ Work toward a faculty that reflects the diversity of the student body

◊ Reconvene in about a year to share the specific initiatives..... undertaken to achieve these objectives

◊ Recognize that this challenge will require significant review of, and potentially significant change in the procedures within each university and within the scientific and engineering establishments as a whole

What the well-meaning academicians who attended the meeting failed to address was the recruitment process for the high-ranking positions. The top jobs are seldom advertised in advance and, if they are, it is well after a favored male candidate is already selected. Yet an official search committee conducts a charade selection process with interviews of prospective unsuspecting female and minority candidates. These deserving candidates actually go through the process oblivious of the hoax, only to be rejected and disappointed later on.

The presidents of the U.S. National Academy of Sciences have all been men since its inception in 1863. According to a

2007 project jointly conducted by the National Academy of Sciences, National Academy of Engineering, and Institute of Medicine, women are being prevented from achieving their highest potential in a male-dominated academic environment.[51] The report reveals the misperception and misrepresentation of women by the privileged men. For example, the common belief that "women are not as good in mathematics and science" is contrary to female performance in high school, which now matches males. The myth that women are "less academically productive" is contrary to the fact that it is now comparable to that of men. And the idea that women are "more interested in family than careers" is contrary to the fact that many women forgo having children and dedicate their lives to their careers.

In the academic world, women are less privileged when it comes to salary and other compensation. In a 2004 published report in the *Annals of Internal Medicine*, it is reported that women not only face barriers to admissions into all academic ranks, but get less compensation than their male counterparts of identical academic ranks.[52, 53]

---

[51]Committee on Science, Engineering, and Public Policy, *Beyond Bias and Barriers – Fulfilling and Potential of Women in Academic Science and Engineering*, 2007. Web. 20 July 2010.
http://www.nap.edu/openbook.php?record_id=11741&page=1#

[52]Christine Laine and Barbara J. Turner, "Unequal Pay for Equal Work: The Gender Gap in Academic Medicine." *Ann Intern Med* 141 (3 Aug. 2004): 238-40. Print.

[53]Arlene S. Ash et al, "Compensation and Advancement of Women in Academic Medicine: Is There Equity?" *Ann Intern Med* 141 (3 Aug. 2004): 205-12. Print.

It was not that long ago that girls and women received compliments such as, "Not bad for a girl," from their male teachers. A few decades ago, some of the females receiving the compliment probably felt flattered. Would they be flattered or offended today? Women are also likely to receive sexually implicit comments from their male colleagues. Almost half the female faculty at medical schools experience some form of sexual harassment. In most instances, complaints against such harassment result in reprisals.[54]

In 2007, a flicker of hope appeared for women in academics at Harvard University. The newly-appointed woman president announced that the university would spend at least $50 million over a decade on initiatives to recruit, support and promote women and ethnic minorities on its faculty. What prompted such drastic measures? A major *faux pas* by the male president of the university. In 2005, he blamed the lack of "intrinsic aptitude" for math and science as a cause for the under-representation of women in those fields. The president ultimately had to resign due to his remark.[55] Is that why Harvard had fallen behind other American universities in recruiting women and minorities.

Under the leadership of a woman since 2006, Harvard has changed. There are more women faculty members, with senior

[54]Phyllis L. Carr, "Faculty Perceptions of Gender Discrimination and Sexual Harassment in Academic Medicine." *Ann Intern Med* 132 (6 June 2000): 889-96. Print.

[55]Scott Jaschik, "What Larry Summers Said." *Inside Higher Ed News.* Inside Higher Ed, 18 Feb. 2005. Web. 15 July 2010. http://www.insidehighered.com/news/2005/02/18/summers2_18

appointments accounting for most of the increase. Even the deans of the engineering school, the law school, the education school, Harvard College and the Radcliffe Institute are now women. The newly appointed dean of the law school had this to say: "This is not your father's Harvard." However, all this progress has a darker side. Harvard lost $11 billion in endowments.[56] The loss of funding is a reflection of who controlled the influx of money—obviously not women.

In the Nordic country of Sweden, men in academics are more privileged than women. A recent survey conducted by the Swedish National Agency for Higher Education revealed that the discrimination of women is "invisible and subtle." Recruitment to attractive posts is not advertised and lacks transparency. This *modus operandi* benefits an exclusive privileged group of men high up in the hierarchy. Furthermore, women are seldom invited to give keynote lectures at conferences and are "excluded from male-dominated informal networks or regularly subjected to derogatory and derisive comments." Such treatments of women are not mere "innocent" episodes, but a clear indication of systematic discrimination and exclusion on the basis of gender.[57]

---

[56]Tamar Lewin, "After Harvard Controversy, Conditions Change but Reputation Lingers." The Female Factor. Education. *New York Times.* New York Times, 5 Mar. 2010. Web. 15 July 2010. http://www.nytimes.com/2010/03/06/education/06iht-ffharvard.html

[57]Högskolenytt för vägledare nr 9, 2007." Högskoleverket. Swedish National Agency for Higher Education, 23 Oct. 2007. Web. 15 July 2010. http://www.hsv.se/aboutus/publications/reports/reports/2005/ covertgenderdiscriminationinacademicarenasinvisiblevisiblesubtle. 5.539a949110f3d5914ec800069154.html

In Japan, too, men enjoy the privilege of higher education, while women and foreigners are often excluded. The country has treated foreigners particularly as separate and unequal. The Korean-Japanese, born and raised in Japan, and, in many cases, second or third-generation Japanese citizens, are still considered "foreigners" and do not enjoy the same rights as "genuine" Japanese citizens. In 1992, the Ministry of Education directed the national universities to *decrease* the number of *gaikokujin kyoushi* or foreign lecturers.[58] Since then, even the well-established and senior, but so-called "foreigners" were terminated, most without prior warning, compensation or pension. As a result, many senior academicians found themselves jobless and unemployable because of their age and seniority.

In sharp contrast, China has set up a degree system, including bachelors', masters' and doctoral programs that are open to foreign students. It has also seen many reforms in higher education since the end of the Cultural Revolution in 1976, when the number of enrollments was a paltry 47,800. In the year 2000, there were only 200 institutions operating under China's ministries. In 2005, there were 4,000 institutions with 15 million students enrolled.[59] Despite such remarkable progress, the needs

---

[58]Charles Jannuzi, "Teaching as a Foreign National at Japanese Universities." *Japan Higher Education Outlook.* 10 Mar. 2008. Web. 15 July 2010.
http://japanheo.blogspot.com/2008/03/teaching-as-foreign-national-at.html

[59]"Higher Education in China." *Wikipedia, The Free Encyclopedia.* Wikipedia, The Free Encyclopedia, 7 Apr. 2010. Web. 15 July 2010.
http://en.wikipedia.org/wiki/Higher_education_in_China#cite_note-Higher_Education_in_China-1#cite_note-Higher_Education_in_China-1

of 85 percent of the college-aged population are not fulfilled, and 70 percent of dropouts in China are girls, and an equal percentage of China's 220 million illiterate are women.[60] Maybe that is why the Chinese government has now started allowing female students to interrupt their studies to look after their children and resume them when their children are older.

In India, the student enrollment in higher education institutions has been increasing rapidly since its independence from the British in 1947—from fewer than 200,000 enrolled in 1950 to almost 7 million in the year 2000 in over 16,000 institutions.[61] However, 304 million of India's population remains illiterate, and only 15 percent of the students finish high school. But most notable is that illiteracy of females is 46 percent—almost twice that of males at 25 percent. Is this because family resources are reserved only for the males so that they may rake in hefty dowries? Or is spending money on the education of females considered a waste because they get married and end up being housewives anyway?

In India, members of the underprivileged ethnic groups have been victims of a host of discriminatory practices. To deal with such discrimination, special categories of the underprivileged

---

[60]Wei Dongbo and Hanghuang Jin, "Comparisons of Special Programs and Policies for Mature Women Students in Canada and China." Proceedings. Hawaii International Conference on Education. 9th Annual Conf. 4-7 Jan. 2011. Web. http://www.hiceducation.org/edu_proceedingsDongbo,percent 20Weipercent20percent20percent20Hanguangpercent20Jin.pdf

[61]"Education in India." *Wikipedia, The Free Encyclopedia.* Wikipedia, The Free Encyclopedia, 15 July 2010. Web. 15 July 2010. http://en.wikipedia.org/wiki/Education_in_India

have been created by the Indian government to promote their advancement in society. These are the Schedule Caste (SC) (the so-called "untouchables,") and Schedule Tribe (ST) (the indigenous people). And just like affirmative action in the U.S., there is a reservation system that guarantees subsidized higher education and job opportunities to the SC and ST. Despite such noble policies introduced decades ago, the meager representation of the underprivileged classes is a reflection of the continued abuse of power by the entrenched privileged. Over a span of two decades, from the late 1970s to the late 1990s, the SC proportion rose from 7 to a mere 7.8 percent, and the ST proportion rose from 1.6 to 2.7 per cent. Of course, there are people opposed to the reservation system because it results in reverse discrimination. Consequently, deserving students from privileged castes who are denied admissions often leave the country and seek higher education overseas. Most never return. But how else can the ills caused by centuries of past discrimination be erased? Perhaps a better solution would be to allow every deserving student to pursue higher education regardless of caste, race or skin color.

For faculty appointments in India, the treatment of the SC and ST is even grimmer.[62] Dr. Phulo Paswan, an SC scholar and also the Chairperson of Department of Maithili, Patna College, Patna University, has witnessed firsthand caste-based discrimination throughout his academic career. He believes that the

---

[62]"Education in India." *Wikipedia, The Free Encyclopedia*. Wikipedia, The Free Encyclopedia, 15 July 2010. Web. 15 July 2010.
http://www.twocircles.net/2008dec25/discrimination_ against_dalits_ higher_education.html

caste discrimination has been unscrupulously practiced through the years. For example, no representative of the SC or ST communities is allowed in the so-called confidential operations of the academic institutions. This failure of the Indian system to promote the advancement of the underprivileged is similar to that of affirmative action in the U.S.—good on paper, but short on delivery.

Under-representation of minorities at academic institutions is multifactorial: fewer graduates, lack of awareness of opportunities, a dearth of mentors and role models, and socioeconomic environmental factors. In India, there is a flicker of hope in the midst of such misguided, exclusionary practices.[63] The government, private industry and some universities are working together to remedy this situation. To that end, the University Grant Commission (UGC) of India directed all the educational institutions to create a separate committee to supervise proper implementation of national schemes meant for the advancement of the minorities and to look into their grievances. One can only hope that once the underprivileged reach positions of authority, they do not abuse their status to discriminate against others out of spite. Mahatma Gandhi once said, "An eye for an eye makes the whole world blind."

---

[63]"Minority Education." Education. Sectors. *National Portal of India.* India.gov, 2005. Web. 15 July 2010.
http://India.gov.in/sectors/education/minority_edu.php

Old Boys' Club in Academic Medicine

In the modern world, academic medicine has been suffering from hierarchies that, over time, has led to disillusionment among young scholars. In an open letter that appeared in the *British Medical Journal* in 2007, 20 young academics from around the world expressed their frustrations with the entrenched culture of "stagnation, compromise, pettiness, opportunism, selfishness, monolithic dogma, and intellectual narcolepsy" that plague the system. In the letter, the authors also stated how they were mere pawns of the "powerful politicians."[64]

Research funding seems replete with powers and privileges that often have little bearing on merit. The established senior scholars in their respective fields have connections and inroads into the funding agencies. A young and deserving independent researcher has a slim chance of acquiring a research grant—unless riding on the coattails of a powerful and well-connected senior scholar. Many times young researchers are expected to spend several years working as research associates of these powerful and well-entrenched academicians in order to make a name for themselves. The senior scholars may have the public believe that the process is all about mentoring. But, behind this façade, one often finds that such mentoring is a sham. Unfortunately, the rules of the game do not change from one generation to the next. The "Old Boys' Club" continues to perpetuate the hierarchies.

---

[64]John P. A. Ioannidis, et al. Open Letter to the Leader of Academic Medicine. *BMJ* 2007, 334: 191-193. Web. 20 July 2010.
http://www.bmj.com/cgi/content/full/334/7586/191

Academia ought to promote excellence, pushing every willing individual to reach his or her full potential. To that end, academic institutions ought to reexamine past performance, openly state their vision for the future, establish concrete steps that will be taken to achieve those stated goals, and last, but not least, conduct periodic reviews of the results. Of course, defining and measuring excellence will be a challenge. While the education of the socioeconomically disadvantaged must not be ignored, leveling the playing field in education must not be achieved by sacrificing the future of other deserving candidates. Only then people—men and women—from all socioeconomic backgrounds are likely to reach their full potential in whatever they choose to do or have a natural inclination for. Art, music, literature, science and mathematics would all fare better if cronyism and nepotism were abandoned, and instead originality and creativity were encouraged.

The Nineteenth Century American poet who is the father of free verse had this to say:

Shut Not Your Doors

Shut not your doors to me proud libraries,
For that which was lacking on all your well-fill'd shelves,
yet needed most, I bring,
Forth from the war emerging, a book I have made,
The words of my book nothing, the drift of it every thing,
A book separate, not link'd with the rest nor felt by the intellect
But you ye untold latencies will thrill to every page.
— Walt Whitman[65]

[65]Walt Whitman – *Leaves of Grass*. Random House, Inc. New York. 2001.

Society as a whole benefits immeasurably from a climate in which all persons, regardless of race or gender, may have the opportunity to earn respect, responsibility, advancement and remuneration based on ability.

– Sandra Day O'Connor (born 1930)
The 102nd and first female U.S. Supreme Court Judge
1981–2005

Chapter 4
Power and Privilege in the Workplace

The workplace is particularly prone to the misuse and abuse of power and privilege. In a modern office setting, a cursory glance around the workplace often reveals the prevalent pecking order: the person making and serving the coffee or spending most of the day at the copier—almost always a female—is probably the least privileged with virtually no power, while the person being served the coffee at the desk and having papers delivered in neatly stacked files, is usually a male and more powerful and privileged in the office. Another giveaway is the attire. A male wearing a dark pinstriped suit and a tie, with a starched white shirt adorned with designer cufflinks, probably enjoys a high degree of power and privilege at the organization. In contrast, employees wearing uniforms wield virtually little or no power as individuals and enjoy very few privileges. The size of the office workspace is another distinguishing factor. The largest, most well-furnished office with views, decorated with expensive artwork and a rug usually belongs to the most privileged and powerful person in the organization. These individuals may also enjoy a private restroom, or an attached full bathroom with shower, a personal refrigerator, a private wet bar, a personal space heater, a *working* thermostat, a pool table, a private workout room, a special covered parking space closest to the building entrance and a company car. Those lower in line often get beat-up lockers in which to place their belongings, a dull and drab common room, and shared restrooms. The housekeeping employees that come in after hours understand the hierarchy in the workplace only too well. They know where not to leave even a speck of dust. Meanwhile, the work areas of the underlings are often ignored and left littered with used coffee cups, empty soda cans, crumbs, dried-up spills, and huge dust balls.

Another common privilege that is enjoyed mostly by men in the workplace is that of being invited to and being heard in important meetings. Women merely enjoy a token presence at such meetings. And if they do make a suggestion or a comment, it is often quickly dispensed with by the mostly male attendees. On many occasions, the same suggestion or comment made by a male member a few minutes later or at a subsequent meeting is regarded as brilliant and original. Maybe this has a physiologic basis; maybe men do not hear the higher pitched female voices very well or have difficulty registering them. Or do the men get distracted to other things about the women?

Executive Powers and Privileges

In large corporations, at the very top is usually the most powerful and privileged individual, the Chief Executive Officer (CEO). Under the direction of the CEO, the chain of command usually consists of vice-presidents (VPs) and senior managers, called the executive staff, with diminishing powers and privileges. As part of their privilege, the CEOs enjoy a host of perks in addition to their lavish salaries. According to *Business Week*, the CEO of a major corporation made 42 times the average hourly worker's pay in 1980, 85 times the average in 1990, and more than 500 times the average by the year 2000. In other words, a CEO earns as much in one day as the average unskilled worker earns in one year.[66]

How else do the CEOs abuse their status? While there were 8 million job losses in the U.S. in 2008 alone,[67] they collected astronomical compensations. Such ruthless insensitivity was exhibited while the average workers were facing layoffs, foreclosures, bankruptcies and homelessness.

There are publicly traded companies that paid their CEO's compensations exceeding U.S. $50 million, while the 2008 Global Recession was well underway. To those who may be more interested, a visit to the AFL-CIO website would be

---

[66]F. John Reh, "CEOs Are Overpaid." *About.* About, 2010. Web. 15 July 2010. http://management.about.com/cs/generalmanagement/a/CEOsOverpaid.htm

[67] Douglas A. McIntyre. "The Layoff Kings: The Companies That Cut the Most in 2008." *24/7 Wall St.* 24/7 Wall St., 20 Dec. 2008. Web. 16 July 2010. http://247wallst.com/2008/12/20/the-lay-off-kin/

highly informative—certainly before investing hard-earned money.[68, 69] According to the 17th annual survey of CEO compensation by the Institute for Policy Studies, 50 firms that laid off workers in 2009 took 42% more compensation, with the average compensation being $12 million.[70] Readers may also find out how the CEOs actually performed by visiting the Forbes.com website and view the ratings of CEO performance.[71]

There are two noteworthy exceptions among such lavish compensations: the CEOs of Apple and Yahoo! They each received $1 each during the same period.

The cancer of astronomical compensations has afflicted some non-profit organizations too. Multimillion dollar annual compensations go to the top executives of notable non-profits.[72]

[68]"Executive Paywatch," AFL-CIO. 2010. Web. 24 Oct 2010.
http://www.aflcio.org/corporatewatch/paywatch/

[69]Douglas A. McIntyre, "The New Wave of Super-Rich Wall St. Executives," *24/7 Wall street.com.* 27 Sept. 2010. Web. 24 Oct 2010.
http://247wallst.com/category/compensation/

[70]Paul Ausick, "CEO Conflict: Layoffs Boost CEO pay," *24/7 Wall street.com.* 1 Sept. 2010. Web. 24 Oct 2010.
http://247wallst.com/2010/09/01/ceo-conflict-layoffs-boost-ceo-pay-c-bac-cat-vz-pfe-emr-jpm-aa-wmt-mrk-jnj-hpq-dis-ibm-t-f-utx/

[71]David M. Ewalt and Nina Gould, "CEO Approval Ratings," *Forbes.com.* 2 May 2005. Web. 24 Oct 2010.
http://www.forbes.com/2003/02/28/cx_dd_0301ceoapproval.html

[72]Amy Bell, "Nonprofit Millionaires." Dec. 2009. Web. 16 July 2010.
http://www.forbes.com/2009/12/17/nonprofits-biggest-salaries-personal-finance-millionaires.html

Some might argue thus in defense of the CEOs: success of the company as well as the overall economy is dependent on the CEOs, and therefore they ought to be generously rewarded. But who decides to give such compensation to the CEOs? It is decided by the powerful members of the Board of Directors. And, who picks the members of the Board of Directors? It is the shareholders and the all-powerful CEO. How many shareholders actually participate in the board elections? Doesn't the "incestuous relationship" afflicting the so-called free market system become obvious? As a result, the corporate world may be in a downward spiral heading toward economic ruin.

Others might argue that there is nothing wrong with astronomical personal wealth accumulation in a free market economy where the sky is the limit. But stop and consider the following in modern society: citizens depend on safe water supply, farming, roads and bridges, ground transportation, air-traffic control, national security and defense, telecommunications, education—including medical education, healthcare, state-funded scientific research and development and state safety regulations, among other things. Who pays the lion's share of the cost of providing all these conveniences in any country? The average salaried middle-income workers pay through the tax on their income, not the super rich. And more important, billions of tax dollars from middle-income citizens have recently helped to bail out distressed companies and banks. Such a culture of privatized astronomical profits, but socialized losses, cannot sustain a free market modern democracy. So would it not be in the best interest of the executives and members of the board to pause and take stock of reality?

In the defense of the CEOs, some may say that their jobs are more challenging today in a global economy than it was a few decades ago. This may be true to some extent. But are the CEOs of today really more qualified or working harder? Do advanced post-graduate degrees from top universities and long working days make them so indispensable? Not necessarily. Billions of dollars have been paid to thousands of incompetent executives who have ruined companies and created massive layoffs. In his 1995 book, *Corporate Executions* (New York: American Management Association, 1995), Alan Downs has shown that CEO salary has a direct and statistically significant relation to layoffs. The table below lists CEO compensations of renowned companies and the layoffs.

CEO Compensation in U.S. $	Number of Layoffs
15,784,831	17,000
9,857,723	35,000
16,626,254	800; expected 10,000 layoffs
17,567,492	20,000
38,237,437	73,000
15,704,585	5,000; dropped 6,000 contracts
16,326,733	3,300
15,460,037	8,000
9,740,471	12,000
42,946,801	3,260
34,031,021	25,000
22,052,273	23,000 jobs lost
25,551,586	850
18,139,878	8,000

Names of the companies available on the website:
http://www.aflcio.org/corporatewatch/paywatch/ceou/database.cfm;

In sharp contrast, no statistical correlation exists between the CEO salary and return on investment.[73] .

The privileges of the top executives are plentiful, with numerous special deals used for lavish payments. There are unique buzz words in the financial world for these executive privileges.[74]

Among the special deals, is the payment of huge sums of money paid to executives at the time of mergers and acquisitions while the jobs of average workers are threatened. Special deals are offered to retiring executives, often to the detriment of the organization. Consider the severance package of the CEO of a home remodeling company who received 210 million dollars at retirement in 2007, not to mention the 123 million dollars he received over the preceding five years as his pay package.[75] All this while full-time workers got laid off and the company's stock performed poorly.

---

[73] "CEO Compensation Index by Company." *AFL-CIO*. American Federation of Labor-Congress of Industrial Organizations, 2010. Web. 15 July 2010. http://www.aflcio.org/corporatewatch/paywatch/ceou/database.cfm;

[74] "Financial Buzz Words." *Investopedia*. Investopedia, 2010. Web. 20 July 2010. [Permission to list the buzz words was not granted] http://stockformation.investopedia.com/categories/buzzwords.asp

[75] "The Home Depot," *Wikipedia, The Free Encyclopedia*. Wikipedia, The Free Encyclopedia. 3 Dec 2010. Web. 4 Dec 2010. http://en.wikipedia.org/wiki/Home_Depot

More recently U.S. citizens were outraged by the astronomical bonuses paid to top executives using TARP[76] money meant to bail-out failed financial institutions. For example, one investment firm gave out 3.6 billion dollars—a third of the TARP money—as bonuses.[77]

Given such excesses, can the top executives be entrusted with the economy?

Fortunately there is hope for a better future. The recent financial regulatory reform introduced by the U.S. government under the leadership of erudite women promises just that. These women, who could never have hoped for partnerships in the financial firms they worked for, nor aspired to earn the eight figure salaries of their male counterparts, will hopefully change the testosterone-driven culture. They are: Mary Schapiro, the head of the Securities and Exchange Commission (SEC) since 2009 [who was called "the Muammar Gaddafi of regulation" by the male insiders]; Sheila Bair, Chair of the Federal Deposit Insurance Corporation (FDIC) since 2006 [who warned bankers in 2007 about the impending crash of the financial markets, but was largely ignored by the males dominating the culture]; and Elizabeth Warren, Chair of Congressional Oversight

---

[76]"Troubled Asset Relief Program," *Wikipedia, The Free Encyclopedia.* Wikipedia, The Free Encyclopedia. 22 Nov 2010. Web. 26 Nov 2010. http://en.wikipedia.org/wiki/Troubled_Asset_Relief_Program

[77]"Merrill Lynch," *Wikipedia, The Free Encyclopedia.* Wikipedia, The Free Encyclopedia. 23 Oct 2010. Web. 26 Nov 2010. http://en.wikipedia.org/wiki/Merrill_Lynch

Panel investigating TARP [who championed the Consumer Financial Protection Agency that the U.S. Chamber of Commerce vehemently opposed but, will ultimately eliminate the hidden traps laid by lending agencies]. While these women are considered outsiders of the financial world, their task will be to "limit and dismantle" the entrenched offenders.[78]

However, the system leaves the investors at a disadvantage. Even if the perpetrators are brought to trial for embezzling millions of dollars of retirement savings, investors get virtually nothing back—despite hefty fines collected from the offenders. Who gets all the money that is collected from such fines? It is certainly not the investors. As a result, senior citizens who have worked hard all their lives are forced to join the work force again, with no hope of ever getting a fair amount of their lost savings back.

What could an average person do to change this blatant abuse of privilege and power? Would such abuse occur if every responsible citizen examined the available facts before applying for a job or even investing in companies that pay such astronomical compensation while laying off workers, or worse yet, while the stock values are declining and the companies are filing for bankruptcy? Can the powerless proverbial beggars of this recent global recession be choosers? Who created this last recession? Did the CEOs? Or, is it the result of society's indifference to the goings-on of corporate culture and government?

---

[78]Michael Scherer -"*The New Sheriffs Of Wall Street*" — *Time* 24 May 2010. Print.

The greed-driven culture can be changed by shifting the emphasis from profits to a more socially responsible business model. How can this be accomplished?

First, the curriculum at business schools around the world needs to be modified. As a start, it must include mandatory classes on topics such as ethics in the business environment and socially conscious policies and procedures.

Then, the top executives and members of the board must re-examine their vision, mission and values. They must have a long-term vision of the future as responsible members of the society and have a mission that not only brings prosperity to the stakeholders but also to society as a whole. And above all, recognize and encourage employee loyalty rather than focus on their bonuses based on quarterly profits stemming from layoffs. It is high time that employee-employer relationships were redefined to bring trust and loyalty back into the equation.

Health Coverage

The privilege of comprehensive health insurance in the workplace is also enjoyed by the privileged and powerful select few. Most top executives enjoy an annual executive physical, while all other employees have deductibles for medical care with other restrictions. Those less privileged may not have paid health insurance at all. It seems to matter little what the economic loss to the company or society may be from lack of healthcare, as long as the CEOs and executives remain fit to collect their astronomical compensations.

Gender and Race Bias

According to a publication titled, *Women's Work, Health and Empowerment* (New Delhi: Aakar Books, 2006), "Women work harder than men, are more likely to invest their earnings on their children, are major producers as well as consumers, and shoulder critical, life-sustaining responsibilities without which men and boys could not survive, much less enjoy high levels of productivity."[79]

Despite the facts, how do power and privilege in the workplace affect women? Compared to their male counterparts, women in westernized countries are seemingly less privileged. In its most simple and commonplace, benign form, a woman does not have the privilege of expressing her anger in the workplace. If she does, no matter what her rank, she runs the risk of being labeled a "bitch" or a "witch." A man, on the other hand, even a low-level worker, can shout and curse, even use foul language, and people will sympathize and say, "He is just having a bad day."

But the preferential treatment of men goes far beyond this simple privilege. For the same work, women have historically been paid lower than men, and their pay continues to lag behind that of men. In the U.S., during the mid-1900s, the practice was so blatantly discriminatory that newspaper advertisements for job listings for men and women were separate—for identical

---

[79]Anjali Gandhi, ed. The book was the result of the recommendations of the 2006 Seminar on 'National Policy of Empowerment of Women' organized by the Jamia Millia Islamia in New Delhi.

jobs—with separate pay. At the time, women with full-time jobs earned approximately 59 to 64 cents for every $1 men earned for identical work. Despite the Equal Pay Act of 1964, today, women continue to get less pay than men for the same work.

In some instances, the pay ratio has slid back since the mid-1990s. For example, in the mid-1990s, women earned 75.5 cents for every $1 in hourly pay to men; in 2005, women earned 74.7 cents for every dollar in hourly pay.[80] The pay difference is even greater for the managers. A notable example is that of Ms. Lilly Ledbetter, a senior manager at a tire manufacturing company, who was paid less than her male counterparts in the company even though she had more experience and tenure.[81]

Most educated working women in the modern Westernized society think they have accomplished everything. The women seem so thrilled with their financial independence and freedoms that they have started to ignore the fight for *real* equality—equality in pay *and* promotions, with equality in representation both in the private as well as the public sector. Luckily there are people in important places who have kept the fight alive. Thanks to the US President, the new Ledbetter Bill of equal pay was amended and signed into law on January 29, 2009. It virtually eliminates the statute of limitations on pay

---

[80]Economic Policy Institute

[81]Ledbetter v. Goodyear Tire and Rubber Co. *Wikipedia, The Free Encyclopedia.* Wikipedia The Free Encyclopedia. 1 Aug. 2010. Web. 24 Sept 2010. http://en.wikipedia.org/wiki/
Ledbetter_v._Goodyear_Tire_percent26_Rubber_Co.

discrimination.[82] What is the guarantee the amended law will work? How will it be enforced? Is there any will in a male-dominated society to enforce it? What hurdles and economic hardships [e.g., lawyers' fees] will the victims encounter to exercise their rights?

When it comes to promotions, women and minorities do not advance as fast as their white male counterparts, and seldom if ever get promoted to the top positions. In the U.S., the Equal Opportunity Act plays a major role in ensuring that women and minorities are given a fair chance to be hired. But the law falls short in ensuring promotions once hired. Even though women constitute 50 percent of the workforce, they are privileged only to hold entry level or low managerial jobs most of their lives; ditto for the minorities. Less than 5 percent of women hold executive positions, and only four of the Fortune 1000 CEO positions are held by women. Even in case of obvious discrimination, women are not brave enough and financially capable to file lawsuits against big companies. Few, however, have dared to come forward, knowing well that there would be serious repercussions. Do such brave women hope to ever get anywhere in their careers?

Women are not as privileged as men to be elected to the Board of Directors. Globally, a paltry 15 percent of Board

---

[82]"Lilly Ledbetter Fair Pay Act of 2009." *Wikipedia, the free encyclopedia.* Wikipedia, the free encyclopedia. 31 Aug 2010. Web. 24 Sept 2010. http://en.wikipedia.org/wiki/Lilly_Ledbetter_Fair_Pay_Act_of_2009

members, including within the Fortune 500 companies, are women, and only 5 percent are senior managers.[83]

Women also abuse their status in the workplace. Some undeserving women get hired, or rise through the ranks faster than other co-workers. The women do so by providing sexual favors to their male bosses. And, when the favors are not duly rewarded, the women bring sexual harassment charges against those men. Who wins in this game? Certainly not the company. Thousands of dollars are lost on legal fees, while employee morale, especially among the women, plummets.

Leave

Is it possible to gauge power and privilege in the workplace by the number of *paid* hours or days off from work? In most instances, the duration of paid leave is directly related to the years of service. This is often true in the public sector. But in the private sector, there are hierarchies. The longer the duration of paid time off, the more privileged the employee within the organization. Of course, the all-expenses-paid business trips and retreats to exotic places in private jets are strictly for the powerful top executive team. Those lower down the line often have to take leave without pay for childbirth or to attend to sick children and elders in the family. Needless to say, such repeated absences from work, either by the fathers or the mothers, are usually to the detriment of future prospects at

[83]Catalyst's Women in Corporate Leadership Study, 1996. Web. 20 July 2010. http://www.pbs.org/newshour/forum/background/jan-june96/catalyst.html

these companies—regardless of superior work ethics and dedication. Does this imply that procreation and caring for the family are incompatible with success in the work environment? Who bears the brunt of these family obligations in most instances? It is usually the women. What can modern society do to create a family-friendly work ethos?

Employees abuse their sick leave privileges too. Surveys suggest that sick leave policy is exploited by 25–40 percent of the employees.[84] Such absences overburden the other employees at work and cause losses to the company. Some employees conveniently take either Mondays or Fridays off to create three-day weekends. Is that why traffic is generally thin on Mondays and Fridays?

Specific Work Sectors

An exploration of specific workplaces should reveal how power and privilege play out and what sorts of pecking orders exist.

In the modern Westernized world, the restaurant business has hierarchical divisions of labor. There is also a hierarchy in the treatment of guests. Behind all the etiquette and formalities, there exists a pattern of implicit policies and procedures. In other words, there are certain unstated privileges, both for the employees and the guests. Workplace privileges in the restaurants are often based on race and appearance, especially in the

---

[84]Patricia Harned, "Abuse of Sick Leave: An Ethical Malad?" *Compliance Week*, 10 Oct 2007. Web. 24 Oct. 2010. http://www.complianceweek.com/article/3697/abuse-of-sick-leave-an-ethical-malady-

high-end restaurants where the powerful dine. Thus, in the U.S., the dishwashers and those who clear the dinner tables are usually not whites, but rather black or Hispanic. They often go about their business as unobtrusively as possible—practically invisible to the patrons. The waiters and waitresses, however, are usually whites. And, since first impressions are important, only good-looking whites become *maître d's*. Their education, work ethic or language skills seem to matter little. For the guests, special privileges become apparent after repeated visits at any given restaurant. The *maître d'*, who wields the power of table assignments gives the choicest tables to the well-to-do as determined by their attire, while tables in less desirable locations, such as those near the kitchen door or near the supply cabinets, are assigned to the less formally dressed.

Another realm of a pecking order in the restaurant business exists in the kitchen. Most chefs are males, even though women have traditionally been the cooks at home for centuries. Is this male presence in the restaurant kitchen a reflection of the more sophisticated skills and palates of the men, or a lack thereof in the women? Are the male chefs more business savvy and more likely to succeed both as employees and as owners? Or, are they preferred on account of the gender bias so pervasive in most other job markets?

In the West, the retail environment is another place one can perceive a hierarchy. This is particularly apparent in the high-end stores. In large superstores, whites usually hold jobs with the most exposure to customers. Meanwhile, jobs performed in the background, such as loading and unloading of merchandise to and from trucks, hauling merchandise from storage to the stands, and carrying away trash, usually go to non-white minorities. Some of these job assignments in the business are also in glaring contradiction to the intelligence, education, work ethic, command of the language and customer relation skills of the workers. Whatever happened to the concept of the best person for the job? Appearances seem to matter the most. Meritocracy seems to be an endangered concept.

In the developing world, in countries such as India, division of labor in the construction industry is skewed in favor of men. The heavy lifting work is done by children and women, often working barefoot, loading bricks and stones into baskets from the storage site; lifting the loaded basket over their heads; and carrying the load to the mason, who may be several floors above ground. Meanwhile, the mason's task of laying the bricks and stones is done by the men. Are Indian women not capable of laying bricks? They can certainly do fine needlework which requires more precision than bricklaying. Also, in this industry, the poor laborers are not even provided with protective helmets or footwear. The working conditions are often extremely hazardous. What is even more ironic is that this practice is so blatant, and yet no one says or does anything to change it. Do families living in their homes think about the labor involved and the unfair treatment of the workers? In fact, most real estate is purchased by the educated, supposedly enlightened and well-meaning upper middle class. Yet, the practice is all-pervasive—perhaps another example of an emotional blind spot.

Developed countries have regulations that protect workers. In the U.S., Occupational Safety and Health Administration (OSHA) was created in 1970, under the Department of Labor. Its creation was considered by many to be "a legislative landmark" that protected workers. But, how many workers are duly protected as dictated by OSHA regulations? How rigorously are the standards enforced?[85]

In the U.S., every April 28 marks Workers' Memorial Day, established to honor and remember those who lost their lives in workplace accidents. Despite OSHA's initial success, the number of work-related deaths has been rising since 2002. In 2006, 5,840 workers were killed on the job. In other words, approximately 16 workers were killed on the job every day. Is this poor performance in the workplace a manifestation of negligence by the workers? Or is it merely an extension of the cancer afflicting the corporate culture where the workers don't matter? Or is it due to the lack of adequate funding of OSHA, poor legal resources, and poor enforcement of safety regulations to effect real change? May be it is all of the above.

Abuse of Workers in the Work Place

The workplace is unsafe due to another little known problem. That problem is bullying. The Workplace Bullying Institute and Zogby International (a leading world market research company based in Utica, NY) conducted 7,740 interviews to

---

[85]U.S. Dept. of Labor. *OSHA*. Occupational Safety and Health Administration, n.d. Web. 24 July 2010. http://www.osha.gov/

create a representative sample of working American adults in August 2007.[86] Following are some of their key findings:

◊ 37 percent of workers (~54 million Americans) have been bullied at work

◊ Most of the bullies are bosses (72 percent)

◊ Women are bullied more than men.

◊ 62 percent of companies ignore the problem

◊ The bullied worker has a 64 percent chance of losing the job for no reason.

Abuse of Social Benefits

Some individuals in modern society abuse social welfare systems designed to help the truly disadvantaged. Unscrupulous con-artists have devised creative ways in which to make money at the tax-payers' expense. The most prevalent ways in which they do so is either by not working at all and enjoying benefits extended to the poor, or by feigning job-related injuries and collecting disability benefits.[87] Do some officers in the welfare department tacitly condone such fraud? What conflicts of interest drive the social workers to abet in the abuse of welfare schemes? Does having a larger number of citizens on social benefits mean job security or higher pay for the officers working

---

[86]Zogby Poll, "As Labor Day Nears, Workplace Bullying Institute Survey Finds Half of Working Americans Affected by Workplace Bullying." *Zogby.* Zogby International., 30 Aug. 2007. Web. 16 July 2010.

[87]Welfare Fraud- Social Security Scam. *Bustathief.com* 2010. Web. 20 Oct.2010. http://www.bustathief.com/welfare-fraud-social-security-scam/

in the department of social welfare? Are there any checks and balances to insure that the tax-funded system is not blatantly abused? In the U.S., citizens can report such fraud by calling a toll-free number: 1-800-269-0271.[88]

Labor Organizations

Workers' unions give its members the tool of collective bargaining. Labor unions facilitate negotiations on wages, work place safety, hiring and firing policies, promotions and benefits, among other things. Contracts agreed upon by unions are often beneficial to its members. But, could collective bargaining capability lead to abuses? Could unions protect the jobs of incompetent and abusive union members? Do union insiders put non-members at a disadvantage in the work environment? Could union leaders abuse their status? How else could the United Auto Workers Union of the U.S. afford to maintain a $33 million lakeside retreat at millions of dollars in annual costs paid by money from union dues? All this in the face of a tax-payer funded $17 billion bailout of the automobile industry in 2008.[89]

[88]Fraud Hotline. *Office of the Inspector General. Social Security Online.* 12 Aug 2010. Web. 20 Oct 2010. http://www.ssa.gov/oig/hotline/index.htm

[89]Autoworkers Union Keeps $6 Million Golf Course for Members at $33 Million Lakeside Retreat – Fox News 26 Dec. 2008. Web. 20 Sept. 2010

Abuse by Government Officials

Abuse of authority by government officials is a global problem. All countries, small and large, rich and poor, have their share of abusive government bureaucrats. Their abuses range from taking bribes to blatant harassment of average citizens. Most citizens accept the excesses, being careful not to anger the officials who wield considerable power and authority. Otherwise, they run the risk of serious, and often unjustified, repercussions. Do citizens have a voice against such powerful government officials? If so, what are the chances that they will get a fair hearing?

The problem is particularly menacing in India. Government officials, across the board, from the local post offices to the nationalized banks treat citizens like cattle. The types of individuals who abuse their status the most are perhaps the least competent. Moreover, most people who gravitate towards government jobs base their decision on their ability to subsidize their income with bribes. Is it any surprise that government officials, including the politicians, in India seem strangely paralyzed to enact or enforce policies that may benefit average citizens? One glaring example is the problem of safe drinking water. As urban populations grow in India, the delivery of a safe and continuous water supply to every household has become a lost dream. City dwellers have to depend on tankers to have their water delivered. Those who can afford to are forced to install storage tanks and water purifiers. This surely seems to have turned into a bonanza for the tanker business, water storing and purifying industry. There is also a booming trade of bottled water. Even though bottled water has a tendency to contain poisons such as pthalates which leach in from the plastic and its transportation consumes millions of barrels of oil every year. In addition, the plastic contaminates the environment.[90] There is no enforcement of state regulations on recycling plastic waste. Why do the government officials and politicians fail to act? Do they not realize that their salaries come from the taxes paid by the average citizens they ignore and abuse? Or do they expect heftier bribes to act?

Another blatant abuse by Indian government officials is in the lack of enforcement of regulations and ordinances in urban development. In New Delhi, India, for example, multi-storey, high density buildings are cropping up in neighborhoods where the ordinances were designed for single or two-family homes. This unbridled construction is going on in blatant defiance of the regulations. Do the state and local enforcement officers fail to notice the illegal construction? Or are they collecting bribes to ignore the problems? Can such unregulated urban development be compatible with quality of life?

Modern Day Slavery

Lately, there has been a trend of women workers from Asian countries such as Bangladesh, India, the Philippines, and Sri Lanka seeking work in wealthier nations, particularly the oil-rich Arab nations. They work usually as domestic servants and night club entertainers (a euphemism for prostitutes). According

---

[90]"Bottled Water" – Natural Resources Defense Council. 25 April 2008. Web. 24 Sept 2010. http://www.nrdc.org/water/drinking/qbw.asp

to the International Labor Organization (ILO), an estimated 1.5 million Asian women are working abroad.[91] The host countries do not allow these women to bring their families with them. Once they leave their home country, these women are powerless, and the home government can do precious little to protect their rights. Also, they do not have any rights in the host country—they are isolated from other people, have travel restrictions, cannot marry a local and cannot change jobs for two years after arriving in the foreign country. In Singapore, they are even subjected to pregnancy tests every six months.

People in favor of such practices might argue that these women are better off working than not working at all, and that their families stand to gain from their work. But can society be served in the long run by such a practice? The proponents fail to realize that the separation of children from their mothers for prolonged periods of time must have a detrimental effect on their normal growth and development. The fathers in these families invariably take to heavy alcohol consumption leading to the deterioration of the moral fiber in society.[92] What will the children from these fractured families be like as adults and parents? Will they be emotionally challenged? Will they be driven to street gangs, crime, or worse yet, be lured to the mercenary terrorist organizations?

---

[91]*ILO.* International Labour Organization, 1996-2010. Web. 23 July 2010. http://www.ilo.org/global/lang--en/index.htm

[92]Barbara Ehrenreich and Arlie Russell Hochschild, eds. *Global Woman: Nannies, Maids, and Sex Workers in the New Economy* (New York: Metropolitan/Owl-Holt, 2004). Print

The ILO does not have the authority to regulate this voiceless and powerless informal sector of labor. In 1990, the United Nations introduced the International Convention on Protection of Rights of All Migrant Workers and their Families.[93] Sadly, only seven member countries have ratified it.

It is even more sad that a poor country, such as India, has not ratified the ILO's convention on home workers. That is because every Indian household, from the middle class and above, depends on domestic servants. Does it come as any surprise that India has not ratified the convention? Furthermore, the Indian Government's Department of Women and Child Development has very ambitious policies that remain mere policies on paper with little in the way of intention and implementation of improving the lot of women and children.[94] Women and children working in this informal/unorganized sector account for almost 60 percent of the Net Domestic Product (NDP).[95] The informal job sector not only includes the domestic servants, but also people who work as animal breeders and farm hands, as artisans, weavers, fishermen, brick makers, stone quarry workers, laborers in the construction and timber industry, as vendors, and in the agricultural sector. According to FAO/

---

[93]"International Convention on the Protection of the Rights of All Migrant Workers and Members of Their Families." *OHCHR*. Office of the United Nations High Commissioner on Human Rights, 18 Dec. 1990. Web. 16 July 2010. http://www2.ohchr.org/english/law/cmw.htm

[94]Anjali Gandhi, ed, *Women's Work, Health and Empowerment.* (New Delhi: Aakbar Books, 2006). Print.

[95]"Net Domestic Product." *Wikipedia, The Free Encyclopedia*. Wikipedia, The Free Encyclopedia, 9 Nov. 2009. Web. 16 July 2010. http://en.wikipedia.org/wiki/Net_domestic_product

UN, in India, a pair of bullocks works 1,064 hours, a man 1,212 hours and a woman 3,485 hours in one year on a one hectare farm. Despite the significant contribution to the economy, these workers enjoy no legislative protection to date. They are poorly paid and have no protection from exploitation. An estimated 836 million Indians make do with less than Rupees 20 per day (U.S. 5 cents).[96] Their daily intake of food is less than that provided to prisoners. Could this factor alone make crime more attractive? In India there are no unemployment benefits or social welfare. While magazine articles and books boast the economic boom of the country, the poor struggle to satisfy basic needs such as food and safe drinking water. Does such abject poverty breed terrorism?

Such deprivation exists in India despite the recent economic boom and projected double digit GDP in coming years. Of course, the countless educated middle class salaried workers stand to gain from such an economic boom. But a nagging question arises. Who is really benefiting from the economic boom? The neo-liberal trickle-down economic policies have benefited the private corporate sector the most. Here is how.

There are 36 super rich Indian businessmen, including the richest family in the world. This small group of Indians accounts for 25 percent of the entire GDP of the country. Furthermore, an estimated 25–45 percent of the GDP exists in the pervasive black market economy. In such a corrupt environment, who are

---

[96]Kamal Nayan Kabra, *High Growth, Rising Inequalities, Worsening Poverty: India's "Development" Experience* (Bangalore, Ind.: Books for Change, 2008). Print.

the corrupt state officials beholden to? To the average taxpayers or people with deep pockets—the super rich and the multinational corporations?

What does the corporate culture look like in a third world country like India? Are Indian executives emulating their greedy counterparts in the West? Indeed they are—even in a country where a significant percentage of the population lives below the poverty line.[97]

There is a growing trend to lift the poor out of poverty by empowering working women. However, the little effort that is made fails because of the entrenched male-dominated culture. For example, the ongoing efforts to promote the financial independence of self-employed women workers by extending micro-credits (e.g., by the Grameen Bank of Bangladesh) has met only partial success in empowering working women.[98] Up to 25 percent of women are forced to pass on all their loans to male family members, and over 60 percent of the loans are actually invested by their male relatives. Could the money lent to the poor working women be siphoned to support extravagant lifestyles and addictions of the male members of the family?

---

[97]Kamal Nayan Kabra, *High Growth, Rising Inequalities, Worsening Poverty: India's "Development" Experience* (Bangalore, Ind.: Books for Change, 2008). Print.

[98]*Grameen Bank* Grameen Communications, 1998, 2010. Web. 23 July 2010. http://www.grameen-info.org/

Approximately 27 million people work as slaves in the world today, most of them children.[99] Even though slavery was abolished in the U.S. in the 1800s,[100] an estimated 14,500 to 17,500 people are currently working as slaves in the country. In addition, each year, foreign nationals, diplomats, state department officers, and officials of international agencies such as the United Nations and the International Monetary Fund (IMF) are permitted to "import" domestic help under special visa categories such as A-3, G-5 and B-1.[101] Approximately 200,000 such visas are issued every year to women from poor nations. These workers have strict restrictions that do not allow job transfers. They also work under constant fear of deportation. Consequently, most of these workers suffer exploitation in silence. In the mainland U.S., most of the victims of slavery are women who come across the southern border seeking a better life. Instead, they are cheated by the traffickers, forced into prostitution or work as domestic slaves.

---

[99]Kevin Bales, "How to Combat Modern Slavery." Talks. *TED.* Technology, Entertainment, Design. TED Conferences, Mar. 2010. Web. 16 July 2010. Video. http://www.ted.com/talks kevin_bales_how_to_combat_modern_slaveryhtml?utm_source= newsletter _weekly_2010-03 31&utm_campaign=newsletter_weekly&utm_ medium=email

[100]"Abolitionism." *Wikipedia, The Free Encyclopedia.* Wikipedia, The Free Encyclopedia, 12 July 2010. Web. 16 July 2010. http:// en.wikipedia.org/wiki/Abolitionism

[101]Barbara Ehrenreich and Arlie Russell Hochschild, eds. "Global Woman: Nannies, Maids and Sex Workers in the New Economy." New York. Henry Holt and Company, LLC. 2002. Print.

Please view the video at the *Free the Slaves* website:

http://www.freetheslaves.net/Page.aspx?pid=356.

In the U.S. administered territories, the situation is even more grim. Notable among them were the sweatshops of the Commonwealth of the Northern Mariana Islands (CNMI), specifically the island of Saipan. According to a 2006 report by Thomas Edsall of the *Washington Post*,[102] an estimated 90 percent of the laborers on the islands were from China, the Philippines, Sri Lanka and Bangladesh. The women were paid less than half the minimum wages by the garment industries established on the islands. Most of these women workers were allegedly forced to work 18 hours a day, were housed in cramped living quarters behind barbed wires, with no facilities such as running water. Some were even forced into prostitution, and if they got pregnant had to undergo abortions. The garments bore the "Made in USA" label, which made their way, "tariff-free and quota-free" to the profitable and famous brand name retail stores in the United States. Did these garments bear any famous brand labels? The answer is yes.[103] What is ironic is that lobbyists in Washington who were paid millions of dollars by the booming garment industry used religion as an excuse to promote their continued operations:

---

[102]Thomas B. Edsall, "Another Stumble for Ralph Reed's Beleaguered Campaign." *Washington Post* Washington Post, 29 May 2006. Wed. 16 July 2010. http://www.washingtonpost.com/wp-dyn/content/article/2006/05/28/AR2006052800964.html

[103]Mark Shields, "The Real Scandal of Tom DeLay." Politics. *CNN.* Cable News Network, 9 May 2005. Web. 16 July 2010. http://www.cnn.com/2005/POLITICS/05/09/real.delay/

spreading the Christian faith amongst these "godless Communist" workers.[104]

The Action Group to End Human Trafficking and Modern-Day Slavery is a US-based organization with the following member organizations:

◊ Carlson Companies

◊ Coalition to Abolish Slavery and Trafficking - CAST

◊ Free the Slaves
◊ International Justice Mission

◊ Not For Sale Campaign

◊ Polaris Project

◊ Ricky Martin Foundation

◊ Solidarity Center

◊ Vital Voices

With the help of such organizations, one can only hope that slavery is replaced by healthy and gainful employment of people all over the world.

Mail-Order Brides

Another abuse of women from poorer nations has a subtle and seemingly civilized form. The women go as mail-order brides to the wealthier nations in Western Europe, Australia, New

---

[104]"Jack Abramoff CNMI Scandal." *Wikipedia, The Free Encyclopedia.* Wikipedia, The Free Encyclopedia, 6 Jun. 2010. Web. 16 July 2010. http://en.wikipedia.org/wiki/Jack_Abramoff_CNMI_scandal

Zealand, North America and Japan to serve older wealthy men—not only to perform all the household tasks, but also to provide sex on demand. Searching the Internet will yield plenty of websites that offer mail-order brides. Men in the Western Hemisphere prefer women from poorer countries because the women are more likely to be "domesticated."[105] Such abuse of women stays well under the regulatory radar screen because it is not considered employment or prostitution. Simply calling the arrangement "marriage" gets a nod of approval from society. The women can only hope that not all the "husbands" are abusive. May be a minority of women do get opportunities to better themselves.

Child Labor

Another major area of abuse of power in the workplace is the exploitation of voiceless and powerless children. Child labor is still prevalent in many parts of the world. In the United States during the mid-1900s, children as young as 7 years of age used to deliver the morning paper in their neighborhoods. Today, older teenagers are seen working in supermarkets after school or during school holidays in the name of acquiring "job experience." Wouldn't their future and the future of the nation be better served by reading and playing? In the developing world, children are employed as factory workers, miners, prostitutes, farm help, tourist guides or as helpers in their parents' businesses; others have their own small businesses (for example,

---

[105]"Mail-order Bride." *Wikipedia, The Free Encyclopedia.* Wikipedia, The Free Encyclopedia, 1 July 2010. Web. 16 July 2010.
http://en.wikipedia.org/wiki/Mail-order_bride

selling trinkets and food), or perform odd jobs for a pittance. Some children are forced to work as domestic servants or in similar informal sectors, in glaring defiance of the labor laws— sometimes in the homes of the regulators themselves.

There were reports of child labor used in the construction of various facilities for the 2010 Commonwealth Games held in New Delhi, India.[106] Did proper living quarters or schools exist for the families at construction sites? Could the poor laborers from a third world country such as India afford day care? Did parents working at these sites ask their children to help basically to keep them from getting into trouble? Such questions are seldom raised and almost never addressed. How many athletes from affluent nations and wealthy spectators even stopped to consider all these questions? Did multinational sporting goods companies that advertised their products at the games or sponsored athletes ever consider the labor involved? How many executives of successful multinationals with regional headquarters in countries such as India, seeking cheap labor, even consider the plight of such children?

In regions plagued by conflicts, children as young as 9 years of age are used as foot soldiers, while others are brainwashed to become terrorists. The use of children as soldiers has occurred in 25 countries around the world. According to one estimate in 1988, approximately 200,000 children have fought wars.

---

[106]Phil Han, "Hard Evidence of Child Labor at 2010 Commonwealth Games." *CNN.* 24 Sept 2010. Web 8 Oct 2010.
http://www.cnn.com/2010/WORLD/asiapcf/09/23/commonwealth.games.child.labor/index.html

Is there a dearth of adults to do the task, or are the children cheaper than having regular armies? The reason is simple. The helpless children do not demand salaries and do as they are told.[107]

According to UNICEF, there are approximately 158 million children, aged 5 to 14, in child labor worldwide—often working as slaves.[108] These numbers do not include child domestic labor and employment in the informal sector.

Despite UNICEF's efforts, the world has developed large emotional blind spots where the abuse of children goes largely unnoticed.

In the 1990s, the Convention on the Rights of the Child (CRC)[109] was formed. The CRC provides international legal *language* prohibiting illegal child labor. However, it fails to make child labor illegal around the world. At its inception, the CRC was ratified by a number of nations: Canada, India, Ireland, New Zealand, Saudi Arabia and the United Kingdom. As of December 2008, 193 countries had ratified it, including every member of the United Nations *except* the U.S. The two reasons often given for the U.S. Senate not ratifying the Convention were that the State of Texas allows children to be given the death penalty (which the Convention does not allow), and that it

---

[107]"Children as Soldiers: The State of the World's Children 1996." *UNICEF.* Web. 20 Oct 2010. http://www.unicef.org/sowc96/2csoldrs.htm

[108]"Why UNICEF." *UNICEF.* United Nations International Children's Emergency Fund, n.d. Web. http://www.unicef.org/why/index.html

[109]"The State of the World's Children." *SOWC.* United Nations International Children's Emergency Fund, n.d. Web. 16 July 2010. http://www.unicef.org/rightsite/sowc/

would undermine parents' rights. This is clearly a manifestation of adultcentrism. In 2008, the US President described the failure to ratify the Convention as "embarrassing" and has promised to review this issue.

What can an individual do to stop such abuse? As a start, an average citizen can help to end slavery by investing in companies that do not use slaves to make a profit. Visit the website:

http://socialinvest.org/

and learn more on how to be a responsible investor.

Ever since the shenanigans of the top executives of Enron,[110] before its tragic demise, and the timely exit of its last CEO from the world stage, one wonders where such sociopathic executives hope to escape? Have they created a paradise for themselves far away from the rest of the world? Have they discovered a secret potion for immortality? Do they not realize that injustices perpetrated today are bound to come back to haunt them? Are they so intoxicated by their short-term success and personal fortunes that they fail to see the destruction of vast segments of society? Could they inadvertently be creating the vigilantes or terrorists of tomorrow by such ruthless insensitivity and unscrupulous attitudes?

What does the modern civilized world have to be proud of besides landing on the moon, eradicating small pox, finding polio vaccine, among other things? The responsible nations of the world have created the United Nations and its various

---

[110]*Enron: The Smartest Guys in the Room* , Dir. Alex Gibney. (Magnolia Home Entertainment. 2005). Film

agencies, such as UNICEF and UNFEM. Granted, the world would be much worse off without them. However, given the extent and magnitude of human abuse of power, these and countless other well-meaning agencies seem like window dressings to hide the darkness within.

❑ ❑ ❑

Real wealth does not come from nothing. Most people have become so desensitized that they only care about their earnings and *perpetual growth* of their personal portfolios, even if it means the environment is left contaminated, the cities are left to rot, vast sections of society are left impoverished, humans are enslaved and war is profitable. Perhaps a look beyond personal short-term profits may help society remain mindful of the far-reaching impact of the present recklessness on people's lives, the environment and world peace.

If hard work were such a wonderful thing, surely the rich would have kept it all to themselves.

— Lane Kirkland (1922–1999)
President of AFL-CIO

Join the union, girls, and together say Equal Pay for Equal Work.

— Susan B. Anthony (1820–1906)
American women's suffrage leader

If men have a right to capitalize their ideas and the resources of their country, then that implies the right of men to capitalize their labor.

— Frank Lloyd Wright (1867–1959)
American architect

Chapter 5
Power and Privilege in Religion

If we are to respect others' religions, as we would have them respect our own, a friendly study of the world's religions is a sacred duty.

— Mahatma Gandhi (1869–1948)
Indian nationalist leader; started the non-violent civil
disobedience campaign to end British rule in India

There is no need for temples [or churches]; no need for complicated philosophy. Our own brain, our own heart is our temple; the philosophy is kindness.

— His Holiness the Dalai Lama (born in 1935)
Spiritual leader of Tibetan Buddhism

Religion is a preeminent societal force affecting human behavior. Religion is not only about faith in the Divine or the importance of the human conscience and consciousness, but also about conformity. And *organized* religion, in particular, has rigid rules of conformity with its attendant hierarchies. It is this aspect of organized religion that can be directly or indirectly blamed for more death and destruction in the civilized world by promoting intolerance and fomenting hatred. It has also been a major contributor to the subjugation of women throughout history. This chapter is a glimpse into some of the organized religions of the world (in alphabetical order).

Buddhism

MALE DOMINANCE: Compared to other major religions, women enjoy a better social status in Buddhism as practiced in Thailand, Sri Lanka, Tibet and Myanmar (formerly Burma). In these Buddhist nations, women are not subjugated as in other religions and are at full liberty to practice their faith. The Buddha himself consoled King Pasenadi when he grieved the birth of a daughter: "A girl may prove even nobler than a son." As a result of just a few wise words of the Buddha, the birth of a daughter is not mourned in the Buddhist faith, and a son is evidently not required to perform the last rites of cremation as is customary in Hinduism. Also, Buddhist women are at liberty to travel alone, without restrictions, unlike in some other religions. Nevertheless, male dominance in the Buddhist cultures is widely prevalent. For example, many Buddhists generally believe that a person is born a woman for committing bad deeds in previous births.

Buddhist women often pray, "May I be reborn as a man in future lives."[111] In Fourteenth Century Thailand, the Queen Mother constructed a monastery and on it is inscribed, "By the power of my good deeds, may I be reborn a man . . ."[112] If there are no religious texts or practices that discriminate against

---

[111]Dominique Side, "Women: A Buddhist View: An Interview with Jetsun Chimey." from *View* Magazine, issue 9. *Rigpa Wiki.* Rigpa Shedra, 16 Aug. 2009. Web. 16 July2010. http://www.rigpawiki.org/index.php? title=Women:_a_Buddhist_ViewpercentE2percent80percent94 An_Interview_with_Jetsun_Chimey

[112]L.S. Dewaraja, "The Position of Women in Buddhism." *Access to Insight,* 5 June 2010. Web. 24 July 2010. http://www.accesstoinsight.org/lib/authors/dewaraja/wheel280.html

women, then did women promote such self-effacing concepts on their own? Or, is male dominance in the religion promoted despite the teachings of the Buddha?

MARRIAGE AND DIVORCE: Buddhists do not consider marriage to be a religious sacrament. It is, in fact, considered a secular matter and does not require religious sanction. Therefore, there are no abuses in domestic life. Divorce is allowed by wives and husbands equally. The divorced women are allowed to keep all their property given to them by their parents at marriage, as well as half of what is acquired during the marriage, plus sufficient money to cover their expenses for six months. After that they have to fend for themselves. Moreover, polygamy, both as polygyny and polyandry, are permitted in some Buddhist cultures.[113]

DEATH AND WIDOWHOOD: In Buddhism, death is considered a natural event in the cycle of life. Thus, widowhood is not dreaded, and widows are permitted to remarry.

LEADERSHIP: In Tibetan Buddhism, there is a male dominated hierarchy.[114] While there are female lamas, the highest position of religious authority rests with the Dalai Lama, the second highest position rests with Panchem Lama and the third highest posi-

---

[113]"Polygamy." *Wikipedia, The Free Encyclopedia.* Wikipedia, The Free Encyclopedia, 13 July 2010. Web. 16 July 2010.
http://en.wikipedia.org/wiki/Polygamy

[114]"Tibetan Buddhism." *Wikipedia, The Free Encyclopedia.* Wikipedia, The Free Encyclopedia, 15 July 2010. Web. 16 July 2010.
http://en.wikipedia.org/wiki/Tibetan_Buddhism

tion with Karmapa Lama. To date, none of these positions of authority has ever been held by a woman. There are indications that the current 15th Dalai Lama is contemplating a female Dalai Lama to lead democracy in Tibet. That would indeed be a refreshing departure from the past

Christianity

MALE DOMINANCE: In the New Testament, Paul, one of the Apostles of Jesus Christ, revealed the status of women in the faith thus:

"Now I want you to realize that the head of every man is Christ, and the head of the woman is man, and the head of Christ is God. Every man praying or prophesying, having his head covered dishonors his [Christ's] head. But every woman who prayeth or prophesieth with her head uncovered dishonoreth her head [her husband]. . . as if she were shaven. If a woman be not covered, let her be shorn. For a man indeed ought not to cover his head . . . he is the image and glory of God; but the woman is the glory of [her] man. For the man is not of the woman, but woman of the man; neither was the man created for woman, but the woman for the man. For this reason, and because of the angels, the woman ought to have a sign of authority on her head."

(I Corinthians 11. 3–10)

Such statements are clearly evidence of the subjugation of women in the Biblical era.

Christianity has many sects. Followers of Catholicism live in communion with the Church in Rome; hence, the followers are called Roman Catholics.[115] The Catholics have canon laws to abide by. The Catholic canon law 1262 (2), issued in 1917, stated, "Men shall be bare-headed when in church or outside a church. . . . Women shall have a covered head and be modestly dressed especially when they approach the table of the Lord."[116] In other words, men dishonored Christ if they covered their heads, but women dishonored their husbands and God if they *did not* cover their heads. Fortunately, in the 1983 promulgation this canon was not reissued. The pendulum seems to have swung so far away from this practice that it is most ironic to see that in modern democratic and secular France, with a Christian majority, female students who wish to cover their heads as a sign of modesty are expelled.

According to some friends who were raised Catholic, their mothers were not allowed to carry the baby to the altar in church at Catholic christening ceremonies. In fact, the baby's mother stayed at home, while the father enjoyed the privilege of participating in the services. This practice was clearly a way of discrediting the contributions of the mother in society.

---

[115]"Catholic Church." *Wikipedia, The Free Encyclopedia.* Wikipedia, The Free Encyclopedia, 16 July 2010. Web. 16 July 2010.
http://en.wikipedia.org/wiki/Catholic_Church

[116]Colin B. Donovan, "Head Coverings in Church." *EWTN.* Global Catholic Network, n.d. Web. 16 July 2010.
http://www.ewtn.com/expert/answers/head_coverings_in_church.htm].

TOLERANCE AND PROSELYTIZING: The Catholic Church denies other Christians the right to call their places of worship churches. For example, the Protestant Christians since the Sixteenth Century have been denied this privilege by the Vatican. These Protestant Christians include the Unitarians, Waldensians, Adventists, Pentecostals and Evangelicals (Calvinists, Presbyterians, Lutherans and Methodists), Quakers and Shakers.[117] All of them consider Jesus as the Son of God and read the same Bible. And yet, the Vatican prefers to call them the Protestant *sects*.

The Roman Catholic Church, instead of adopting a conciliatory and egalitarian approach to other religions and "sects" of the world, conducts itself with a certain degree of arrogance. As recently as 2006, the Pope made a statement (which later had to be clarified) about Islam as "evil and inhuman" and a faith "spread by the sword." Perhaps a short course in the history of the Crusades of the Twelfth Century may be in order, where holy wars were fought against Muslims, pagans, Russian and Greek Orthodox *Christians*, Mongols, Cathars and all "enemies of the Pope."[118] Hundreds of thousands of lives were lost while "spreading" Christianity. The Twenty-First Century War on Terror is perceived by some Muslims as another such holy war. How can this paranoia be erased? How can we stop Muslim men—even those with modern scientific education—

---

[117]"Protestantism." *Wikipedia, The Free Encyclopedia*. Wikipedia, The Free Encyclopedia, 14 July 2010. Web. 16 July 2010.
http://en.wikipedia.org/wiki/Protestantism

[118]"Crusades." *Wikipedia, The Free Encyclopedia*. Wikipedia, The Free Encyclopedia, 16 July 2010. Web. 16 July 2010.
http://en.wikipedia.org/wiki/Crusades

from going to training camps for Jihad? It may be prudent for *all* religions to clearly restate and re-emphasize the real goals of the War on Terror. And, more important, have all Muslim nations play a more active role in the anti-terrorism efforts rather than merely offering lip service to the cause while sheltering the terrorists.

An extension of Christian proselytism is the placement of the Holy Bible in almost every hotel and motel room by Gideon International, a charitable evangelical Christian organization— even in the secular democratic nations that have a Christian majority.[119] Is the reason behind the placement of the Holy Bible in every room to spread Christianity and save humanity, or is it giving the Christians the privilege of having their holy book available even when traveling? One has to wonder how the Christian guests of the hotel would react if they were to find copies of the holy books of other world religions: the Holy Qur'an [Islam], the Bhagavad Gita [Hindu], the Torah [Judaism] or the Guru Granth Sahib [Sikh]. And, how the guests would react if, based on their faith, they were given a choice of their holy book at check-in, just as they are given the choice of smoking or non-smoking rooms? And what if in communist China guests saw copies of the little Red Book in their hotels? It might be a good idea to place copies of the U.S. Bill of Rights (or its equivalent) to remind people of the wisdom contained therein, and spread secular democracy and freedom of speech on the planet. Since so many wars are

---

[119]"Gideons International." *Wikipedia, The Free Encyclopedia*. Wikipedia, The Free Encyclopedia, 18 Oct. 2010. Web. 20 Oct 2010.
http://en.wikipedia.org/wiki/Gideons_International

fought in the name of religion, wouldn't reading religious books of other faiths encourage reconciliation and world peace? After all, the aim of reading such books is to feel close to God.

LEADERSHIP AND ABUSE OF POWER: The Catholic Church is organized globally into ministries run by *men* ordained into three levels of hierarchy: the Pope, the College of Bishops and parish priests. These largely deserving devout men are ordained, no doubt by a line of similarly ordained elders that dates back to the Twelve Apostles. But only men enjoy the privilege of being so ordained. The women who join the Catholic Church as nuns, and who are eminent scholars of the Holy Bible, lead the most devout and austere lives, shrouded virtually from head to toe in "veils," do not qualify. Even the most recent canon released by Pope John Paul II in 1994 re-emphasized the Church's stance on not ordaining the nuns.

Why are women denied the privilege to be ordained in the Roman Catholic Church? Consider this quote from the Holy Bible:

> *A certain woman of the company lifted up her voice*
> *and said unto [Jesus], "Blessed is the [mother]*
> *that bare thee, and the paps which thou has sucked."*
> *But He [Jesus] said, . . . "Rather, blessed are they*
> *that hear the word of God and keep it."*
>
> (Luke 11:27–28.)

If Jesus himself discredited his own mother in this way, there is little wonder that the Vatican still maintains its males-only policy regarding ordination. So it is unlikely the world will see a female Pope in the near future.

In contrast, the Church of England is the *Mother* Church and the oldest of the worldwide Anglican Communion.[120] Followers consider themselves both Catholic and Reformed. This is done out of respect for the Church of Christ in unbroken continuity with the original Apostles and the medieval church, as well as the Sixteenth Century Reformation. The Church of England ceased to be under papal authority in 1534. It has a Book of Common Prayer. In contrast to the Roman Catholic Church, the Church of England started appointing women as ministers during the First World War. Was this shift in the "male only" policy a reflection of the wisdom of the male leaders of those times? Not quite. The decision was one of necessity, an emergency measure due to the shortage of men during and after the war. It was nonetheless a significant step toward equality of the genders. Unfortunately, these ordained female priests were called "Bishop's Messengers;" the bishops were always men. It was not until 1992 that the concept of ordaining women was first considered and duly accepted in 1994. By 2008, women could be ordained as bishops too.

The Roman Catholic churches are centrally controlled from the Vatican, without local governance. This distance between the central authority and various parishes has, over time, led to abuses by the powerful and privileged clergy in their communities.

---

[120]"Church of England."*Wikipedia, The Free Encyclopedia.* Wikipedia, The Free Encyclopedia, 10 July 2010. Web. 16 July 2010.
http://en.wikipedia.org/wiki/Church_of_England

In Fourteenth Century Spain, local abuse of power by the priests took on a sinister form. The Jews—even those who converted to Catholicism—were believed to have "bad blood" (*mala sangre*) inherited through generations, and were subjected to torture, humiliation and expulsions.[121] This persecution brought the golden age of Jewish culture in Spain to a tragic end.

Most notable among abuses of power in the Catholic Church is the sexual assault of children by priests. The Church has been infiltrated by pedophiles over the years. A recent nine-year investigation in Ireland unveiled the systematic abuse of abandoned children while under the guardianship of the Catholic Church. The children, mostly boys, were sexually abused and beaten. The Church had full knowledge of the presence of pedophiles in the rank and file of their churches worldwide, as well as the abuse of boys, but did precious little to stop the practice.[122] How long has this been going on? Only recently did the victims of the abuse, now adults in their 50s to 80s, speak out in public. They lobbied long and hard for an official investigation. Finally, towards the end of the Twentieth Century, and after civil lawsuits in the U.S. and the 2005

[121]"History of the Jews in Spain." *Wikipedia, The Free Encyclopedia.* Wikipedia, The Free Encyclopedia, 9 July 2010. Web. 16 July 2010. http://en.wikipedia.org/wiki/History_of_the_Jews_in_Spain

[122]Abuse Tracker. *Bishop Accountability.* Web 20 July 2010. http://www.bishop-ccountability.org/AbuseTrackerArchive/2010/05/Web 20 July 2010.

Fern Report in Ireland, did the Church finally admit wrongdoing and publicly apologize.[123] Reports of sexual abuse by clergy are also surfacing in Germany; some reportedly having occurred during the period when the current Pope Benedict XVI was the Archbishop.[124] In the year 2000, Pope John Paul II asked for forgiveness ". . . for the sins of Catholics throughout the ages." Perhaps the recognition of the abuses of power by the clergy was at the center of his prayer.

Hinduism

Before delving into the rules of the religion, a clarification is in order. Contrary to common belief, Hinduism is not polytheist. According to the Vedanta philosophy, Hindus believe in *one* God.[125] This Vedic Hindu tenet takes the faith in one God a step further than the monotheist mainstream religions: Divine and *Self* are One. In other words, there is no separate God, residing in Heaven, to be feared, revered, or loved. The Divine resides in everything; the human body is but one of countless temples. However, over the centuries, Hindus created symbols (e.g., the Swastika, the OM), and superhuman

[123]Francis D. Murphy, Helen Buckley, and Larain Joyce, "The Ferns Report." *Bishop Accountability*. Web. 16 July 2010.
http://www.bishop-accountability.org/ferns/

[124]Nicholas Kulish and Rachel Donadio, "Abuse Scandal in Germany Edges Closer to Pope." Europe. *New York Times*. New York Times, 12 Mar. 2010. Web. 16 July 2010.
http://www.nytimes.com/2010/03/13/world/europe/13pope.html

[125]"Advaita Vedanta." *Wikipedia, The Free Encyclopedia*. Wikipedia, The Free Encyclopedia, 27 Jun. 2010. Web. 16 July 2010.

idols to have something tangible to worship, often portraying God as having supernatural powers (much like the modern-day fictional creations of Superman and Spiderman). Consequently, there are literally thousands of Hindu deities. There is a common Indian saying, "There are as many forms of the Divine as there are rocks on the planet." And, just as many rituals.

The Hindus have a holy book called the Bhagavad Gita which most consider to be their bible.[126] The Gita is a small part of a mythological epic believed to have been composed by Vyasa around Fifth Century, BCE. It narrates the conversation between a warrior [Arjun] and his charioteer, Krishna, God incarnate. The verses basically teach the importance of doing one's duty in life without attachment, and knowing that the material world and the body are illusions, while each soul is the eternal part of the Divine. Nevertheless, despite such philosophical teachings of the Gita, there are hierarchies in the religion that are more than mere illusions.

MALE DOMINANCE: According to the ancient Hindu scriptures, "The deathless Self has no gender, caste nor race. The Self is changeless and infinite, the source of life, and [a part of the] Divine that is above name and form, and is present in all and transcends all." So, to Hindus, the Divine is not always male as in most other religions. The Hindu scriptures do not always address the Divine as "He, our Lord and Master." The

---

[126]"Bhagavad Gita." *Wikipedia, The Free Encyclopedia.* Wikipedia, The Free Encyclopedia, 31 Aug. 2010. Web. 2 Sept. 2010.
http://en.wikipedia.org/wiki/Bhagavad_Gita

Divine can be a Goddess Mother—She, our Lady—with as many names and qualities as there are mothers in the world; often portrayed with multiple arms, capable of multitasking like most mothers. Even the mythological male deities worship the Divine Mother. The Vedas also mention women religious scholars. Hindu women who chose sagacious lives could perform rituals in temples. Interestingly, the Vedas have a marriage hymn that says, "I am the banner and head, a mighty arbitress am I. I am victorious, and my Lord shall be submissive to my will."[127] Thus, in ancient Hinduism, women held an honorable position.

Yet, somehow, over the centuries, male hierarchies have emerged in Hindu societies, and the status of women has deteriorated. How did this change come about? They lost that honorable status around 1200 BCE, when a sage named Manu compiled laws for the Hindu community to follow.[128] This compilation is called Manav Dharma Shastra (or Shastra), and was considered a standard canon of Hinduism, which defined a Hindu way of life. The laws were contained in over two thousand verses, divided into 12 chapters; they pertained to the domestic, social and religious life in the subcontinent. Manu's Shastra did a huge disservice to Hindu women. For the first time, women were denied their right to learn the

---

[127]"Vedas." *Wikipedia, The Free Encyclopedia.* Wikipedia, The Free Encyclopedia, 14 July 2010. Web. 16 July 2010.
http://en.wikipedia.org/wiki/Vedas

[128]"Manusmriti." *Wikipedia, The Free Encyclopedia.* Wikipedia, The Free Encyclopedia, 11 July 2010. Web. 16 July 2010.
http://en.wikipedia.org/wiki/Manu_Smriti

scriptures and have an independent spiritual life; Manu even spread the belief that women were evil and sinful and could reach heaven only through devout obedience to the husband. His misogynistic views had a lasting impression on Hindu society.

Women were further disadvantaged by the Shastra, which states that the last cremation rites should only be conducted by the son of the deceased. Only then would the deceased get a place in Heaven. This pronouncement was not made out of sympathy toward the soft-hearted women so as to spare them the heart-wrenching duties of cremation. It was designed to subjugate them. By simply barring women from performing the funeral rites on their deceased family members, including their parents, husbands, and children, they were rendered worthless in this regard, and the sons became indispensable. Consequently, even today, families strive to have at least one son who can perform the last rites. This is one reason why the birth of a boy is celebrated by Hindu families. Their place in heaven is assured—even if they kill all their daughters.

The Shastra also introduced ownership and inheritance laws, further putting women at a disadvantage. Women were allowed to own property (*Stridhan*), but it was not considered sacrilegious to pilfer it. Thus, with increasing subjugation of women over time, husbands began to lay claim to their wives' possessions at will, leaving them financially dependent. In the laws of inheritance, the daughter was privileged to inherit all her mother's property—that is, if there were any belongings left untouched by the men of the household. In Hinduism, all the sons got three quarters of the family inheritance; the daughters shared the remaining quarter. Some men would argue that this unequal division of inheritance was fair because some of the family savings were given as dowry at the time of the daughters' marriage.[129]

MARRIAGE AND DIVORCE: The Shastra also introduced different set of rules for divorce. The wives could be divorced "Immediately if they be found disobedient, diseased or disfigured, or after eight years if they do not produce male heirs, and after 11 years if all their children die." Meanwhile, the women were betrothed for life, even if the husbands were blatantly adulterous and abusive. The subjugation of women was further exacerbated by the practice of child marriages so that men could have young girls as wives.[130]

WIDOWHOOD: According to the Shastra, a widower could remarry at will, while a widow could remarry *only* if she were still a virgin, childless or had no brother-in law (*devar*)[131] to serve. But if she had brothers-in-law, she lived as their slave for the rest of her life. And if she did not have brothers-in-law, or was not a virgin, she was left to begging in order to survive. Because of this sorry plight of widows, they were treated as outcasts in the community, barred even from entering temples or attending religious ceremonies. They were forced to wear only white clothes so that they could be easily identified.

---

[129]"Dowry." *Wikipedia, The Free Encyclopedia.* Wikipedia, The Free Encyclopedia, 12 July 2010. Web. 16 July 2010.
http://en.wikipcdia.org/wiki/Dowry

[130]"Child Marriage." *Wikipedia, The Free Encyclopedia.* Wikipedia, The Free Encyclopedia, 11 July 2010. Web. 16 July 2010.
http://en.wikipedia.org/wiki/Child_marriage

[131]in Hindi the word literally means second husband

Another form of female subjugation was the practice of "voluntary" death at funerals. It had been a prevalent practice in northern India before 200 BCE.[132] The practice was similar to *Seppuku* the voluntary disembowelment of Samurai in Japan.[133] Apparently such suicide was also practiced in Scythia, Egypt, Scandinavia and China.[134] The original practice in India had many names: *anumarana, jauhar,* or s*aka*, and was practiced by the surviving partner, or when faced with defeat in a war to avoid capture and dishonor at the hands of their enemies. The practice was popular among the Hindu and Sikh women during Mughal (Muslim) rule. The most notable example of mass self-immolation took place after the defeat in battle against the Muslim invaders in western India, where thousands of Rajput women set fire to themselves (jauhar) to escape the horrors of genocidal rape. Sporadic cases were also reported during the Partition of India in 1947, when women preferred death by self-immolation to being raped, becoming domestic sex slaves, or being forced to marry and adopt their captors' religion.

---

[132]Sati (practice). *Wikipedia, The Free Encyclopedia.* Wikipedia, The Free Encyclopedia, 27 Jun. 2010. Web. 16 July 2010.
http://en.wikipedia.org/wiki/Sati_(practice)

[133]"Seppuku." *Wikipedia, The Free Encyclopedia.* Wikipedia, The Free Encyclopedia, 27 Jun. 2010. Web. 16 July 2010.
http://en.wikipedia.org/wiki/Sepukku

[134]"Self-immolation." *Wikipedia, The Free Encyclopedia.* Wikipedia, The Free Encyclopedia, 3 July 2010. Web. 16 July 2010.
http://en.wikipedia.org/wiki/Self_immolation

This practice of self-immolation was voluntary and not restricted to widows. Anyone, male or female, with personal loyalty to the deceased could commit "suicide" at a loved one's funeral pyre. Sometimes these included the relatives of the deceased, servants, followers, or friends. However, in India, over the centuries, when the practice was *imposed* on widows; it was called *Sati*. Even though it was supposed to be voluntary when first introduced, it is known that widows were forced, often tied down or pushed onto their husbands' funeral pyres. Who did the pushing? It could not possibly be the women of the family, because they were not allowed to attend the cremation ceremonies. One wonders what purpose forced *Sati* served. Did the men in the family want to claim the deceased man's assets? Did they consider a widow a financial burden or accursed in some way? What was the plight of the orphans? And, what if the widow were pregnant or nursing a baby? Did they keep the baby boy and throw the baby girl onto the pyre with the mother? Of course there cannot be straightforward answers. The practice bordered on cold-blooded murder. There are sporadic cases of *Sati* reported in India even today—despite laws banning the practice.

LEADERSHIP AND ABUSE OF POWER: One of the consequences of Manu's Shastra was the creation of four sects (*varna*) in a society based on the skills and tasks performed by individuals in a community.[135] Much like the modern-day professional societies such as the American Medical Association,

---

[135]"Varna (Hinduism)." *Wikipedia, The Free Encyclopedia*. Wikipedia, The Free Encyclopedia, 12 July 2010. Web. 16 July 2010.
http://en.wikipedia.org/wiki/Varna_(Hinduism)

Trial Lawyers Association, Royal College of Physicians, etc., these *varnas* were designed to identify individual expertise within one of four categories, in alphabetical order: 1) scholars of religious scripture, teachers, and priests were called *brahmins*; 2) warriors and rulers were called *kshatriyas*; 3) unskilled laborers were called *shudras;* 4) farmers, merchants, and traders were called *vaishyas*. This division of society into *varnas* was the forerunner of the caste system which is still prevalent in modern India. An individual was usually born into a particular *varna*. But flexibility of adopting other trades or expertise was allowed. Thus, an individual could be born a *shudra*, but after learning the scriptures could become a *brahmin* by deeds (*karma*).

The caste system is so entrenched, that even Christian converts identify themselves as Christian *brahmins* or Christian *shudras*. Over time, this division of society into *varnas* gradually led to elitism and bigotry. Worse yet, the *brahmins* started to abuse their positions and used their influence over the rulers to create privileges for their *varna*. They elevated themselves above all other sects, even above the law, so that they could not be punished for their crimes. This privileged status was very similar to that of the Catholic priests during the Inquisition of Fifteenth Century Europe.[136] Furthermore, contrary to the teachings of the *Vedas*, the *brahmins* barred the *shudras* from entering temples and participating in rituals. This led to the oppression of the unskilled workers, and the creation of the despicable practice of "untouchability," which continues to plague Indian

---

[136]"Inquisition," *Wikipedia, The Free Encyclopedia*. Wikipedia, The Free Encyclopedia, 29 Oct. 2010. Web. 29 Oct. 2010.
http://en.wikipedia.org/wiki/Inquisition

society. Today, the untouchables call themselves *Dalits*. Even though the practice of untouchability was outlawed after Indian independence in 1947, the law was never enforced. Fortunately, education is changing the treatment and perception of these individuals in India. There have been two *Dalit* Presidents since independence; there are *Dalit* members of Parliament, including cabinet Ministers; and *Dalit* scholars. But change is painfully slow to come to the small towns and villages of India.

To protect their elite privileged status, the *brahmins*, over the centuries, made themselves indispensable by introducing elaborate (and often wasteful) religious rituals that only they could perform—of course, in return for rewards. Such rituals are still performed in temples throughout India. The rituals have precious little to do with understanding the Divine within. On the contrary, they are focused on a separate Divine without.

PROSELYTIZING AND TOLERANCE: The *brahmins* enforced the concept of being *born* into a particular *varna*. This was contrary to the original intent. Did the *brahmins* want to restrict and preserve their privileges in the communities? Is that why proselytizing was discouraged in Hinduism? Luckily, there is no central authority like the Vatican in Hinduism. And according to the Shastra, no one can be barred from becoming a Hindu.

Islam

MALE DOMINANCE: In the holy book of Islam, the Holy Qur'an, there are 99 names or attributes of God.[137] Some of these attributes include the Compassionate, the Merciful, the Absolute, the First, the Last, the Resurrector, the Light, the Judge, the Forgiver, the Cause of Life and Death, the Creator, the Protector . . . and the list continues. Many of these attributes of the Divine are recognized by the Hindus, with their own selection of Sanskrit names.

The Holy Qur'an was compiled from quotes of the Prophet Mohammed, who is believed by his followers to have received divine revelations throughout his life. It states "Men and women were created from a single soul." Here is what Mohammed had to say when asked a question:

> *"Whom shall I honor the most?"*
> *The Prophet replied: "Your mother."*
> *"And who comes next?" asked the man.*
> *The Prophet replied, "Your mother."*
> *"And who comes next?" asked the man.*
> *The Prophet replied, "Your mother!"*
> *"And who comes next?" asked the man.*
> *The Prophet replied, "Your father."*
>
> (Sahih Bukhari 8.73.2)

---

[137]"Names of God in Islam." *Wikipedia, The Free Encyclopedia.* Wikipedia, The Free Encyclopedia, 7 July 2010. Web. 16 July 2010. http://en.wikipedia.org/wiki/99_Names_of_Allah

As a result of His teachings, mothers enjoy a very privileged and honorable status in Muslim society. In the days of Mohammed, the status of women was at par with pets. Thanks to Mohammed, women could enjoy a respectable status in society. Mohammed was clearly way ahead of His time—even further ahead than the Muslim clerics of modern-day Islam. Unfortunately, however, His words have been distorted over the centuries, and the status of women has gradually deteriorated. Today it seems as though the Holy Qur'an is misinterpreted to promote male dominance.

Most societies of those times did not grant any inheritance to women. Before Islam, women were regarded by the prevailing cultures as any other piece of property—belonging to their fathers before marriage and to their husbands or sons thereafter. The Holy Qur'an, for the first time, spelled out inheritance laws with a share for women—more than a millennium before Europe even considered the issue for debate.[138] Muslim women got the right to own, for the rest of their lives, what they received at the time of marriage; it was a sin for the husband or the sons to lay a claim on it. However, in Islam, the men get a larger share of inheritance. They are supposed to get twice as much as the mothers, wives, daughters and sisters. The justification there is that men have greater financial obligations than women, and that women get a lump sum at their marriage from their fathers.

---

[138]"Women in Islam." *Wikipedia, The Free Encyclopedia*. Wikipedia, The Free Encyclopedia, 13 July 2010. Web. 16 July 2010.
http://en.wikipedia.org/wiki/Women_in_Islam

The dress code in Islam is one aspect where the Holy Qur'an seems to have been grossly misinterpreted by men to suppress women. It clearly states thus: "Believing women should lower their gaze and guard their modesty . . . and draw their veils over their *bosoms* . . ." It does not state that they should cover their heads and faces, wear gloves and be confined to the house, and never to leave home without a male escort. The Holy Qur'an also states: "Wives and daughters and the believing women should cast their outer garments over their bodies so that they should be known and *not molested.*" [Emphasis is added]. Have the men misinterpreted this? Is the current version of the full veil being worn by the women to protect them from molestation? Does this misinterpretation lead the men of Islam to believe that women who are not covered by the veil are fair game? Perhaps these men ought to re-read the Holy Book and abide by it wherein it clearly states: ". . . lower your gaze when in mixed company."

Education of women was once encouraged in Islam. They were not barred from learning—not even the learning of the Holy Qur'an. In the Twelfth and Thirteenth Centuries, Damascus (Syria) boasted more than two dozen educational institutions for women. Women were privileged to earn *ijazahs* (degrees), and qualified as scholars and teachers, centuries before modern day Western society admitted women to educational institutions. Women were even allowed to work outside the home as long as they maintained their modesty and their safety was not compromised. There were 8,000 women jurists, and 15 percent of scholars were women. Today, there is not a single female jurist in an Islamic nation.[139] At what point in time did Muslim women in some countries stop getting an education and why? Keeping women ignorant seems to be a part of the male Muslim agenda. In 2009, the Director of Baghdad's Displacement Committee suggested that all property owned by widows ought to be placed in the care of men who offered to marry them.[140]

One of the most glaring examples of the subjugation of women pertains to rape. According to the Sunni Hadith [canon], rape (zina) is punishable by death, but the victim has to produce four (male) witnesses.[141] Consequently, few cases, if any, get reported and prosecuted. And if they do get reported, the victim invariably gets severely punished. Meanwhile, punishment for the man is varied and depends upon the discretion of the presiding judge. This has been a point of contention among scholars of Muslim women's rights. Liberal Muslims and Islamic feminists are encouraging debate on how to extend Qur'anic laws to modern society and treat women with respect and equality.

---

[139]Carla Power, "A Secret History." *NY Times.* The New York Times, 25 Feb. 2007. Web. 16 July 2010.
http://www.nytimes.com/2007/02/25/magazine/25wwlnEssay.t.html

[140]*TIME* Magazine – 9 Mar. 2009

[141]"Zina (Arabic)." *Wikipedia, The Free Encyclopedia.* Wikipedia, The Free Encyclopedia, 7 Jun. 2010. Web. 16 July 2010.
http://en.wikipedia.org/wiki/Zina

Another example of unfair treatment of women pertains to prostitution. Islam permits temporary marriage (*Nikah al-Mut'ah*)[142], duly sanctioned by a cleric. This arrangement gives prostitution religious sanction and a moral face. The exploited women often hail from poor rural areas and have no other means of surviving in big cities. The men who recruit their services lead normal respectable lives, but the women live in disgrace. Their plight is dismal at best. Furthermore, what is the fate of children born to these women? Perhaps it may be time for religious scholars to include new canons on the subject, so that the women who devote their lives to this invaluable "profession" are not only compensated duly for their services, but are treated with the utmost respect befitting mothers, sisters and daughters. After all, these women are, at some point in their lives, any one of the three.

MARRIAGE AND DIVORCE: Divorce is a privilege of men and women, among both Shi'ite and Sunni Muslims. This can easily be achieved by stating the word *Talaq* three times; the word means, "I divorce you." At the time of divorce, the Muslim man is supposed to give back the wife's property, and pay child support until the baby is weaned. In addition, the divorced woman receives one year's support from her husband's estate. After this initial support period, the women have to fend for themselves. But divorced women cannot live alone. Consequently,

---

[142]Nikah Mut'ah. *Wikipedia, The Free Encyclopedia.* Wikipedia, The Free Encyclopedia, 3 Sept. 2010. Web. 4 Sept. 2010.
http://en.wikipedia.org/wiki/Nikah_mutah

they are forced to return to their parental home.[143] And if those doors are closed, and if the divorce is without an education, these women take up begging as a means of survival. The same fate befalls widows. Fortunately, Islam permits remarriage of divorced women and widows.

Widowhood is not dreaded in Islam as it is in Hinduism. A woman has to wait four months and ten days after the death of her husband before she can remarry.

Polygamy was and still is practiced in many parts of the world. In the Old Testament, there is clear indication that it was customary to have more than one wife, where the Jewish Talmud allowed a maximum of four wives. The Jews practiced polygamy in Europe until the sixteenth century. In Africa, it is still widely practiced by men of different religions.[144] It was only under the influence of both the Greeks and Romans that the practice began to fade.

Mohammed addressed the issue of polygamy after the battle of Uhud where many Muslim men died in battle:[145]

---

[143]"Talaq." *Wikipedia, The Free Encyclopedia.* Wikipedia, The Free Encyclopedia, 13 July 2010. Web. 16 July 2010.
http://en.wikipedia.org/wiki/Talaq_(Nikah)

[144]"Polygamy."*Wikipedia, The Free Encyclopedia.* Wikipedia, The Free Encyclopedia, 13 July 2010. Web. 16 July 2010. http://en.wikipedia.org/wiki/Polygamy

[145]Mohammed Marmaduke Pickthall, *The Meaning of the Glorious Koran: An Explanatory Translation* (New York: Mentor-New American Library, n.d.). Print.

Give unto orphans their wealth. [Do not] absorb their wealth into your own. . . . And, if you fear that you will not deal fairly with the orphans, marry women, two or three or four to do justice [to them all]. (Surah IV)

There are many such enlightened statements regarding the treatment of widows and orphans made by Mohammed contained in the *Surah IV.* But the real intent of Mohammed in helping orphans and widows seems to have been lost over the centuries. According to 2007 UNICEF estimates, there are approximately 145,000,000 orphans worldwide.[146] The total world population of Muslims is 1,480,083,062. If one considers half of that number to be men, then that would mean there are roughly 740,000,000 Muslim men in the world. If each Muslim man adopted five orphans (as advised by Mohammed), and then took on four or more wives to look after them, the world would not have any orphans. The divine word of the Prophet would be honored, and the whole world would be in awe of the greatness of Islam. Why don't the clerics preach such philanthropic concepts as clearly stated in the Holy Qur'an?

Unfortunately, Muslims today, including the Imams (Caliphs), have interpreted the Prophet's words unwisely and unjustly. Contrary to Qur'anic prescription, Muslim men take on more than one wife *neither to help raise orphans, nor to help the plight of widows.* Instead, they consider it their privilege to marry young brides—as long as the first wife grants permission to do so. And if she does not grant permission, she runs the risk of being falsely accused of infidelity and stoned to death.

---

[146]Jed Medefine, "Global Orphans: The Numbers." *Christian Alliance.* 25 July 2009. Web. 20 Oct 2010. http://chrisitianallianceblog.org/?p=74

According to Sharia law, marriage cannot be forced. And, yet, young Muslim girls from poor families in developing countries such as India, Pakistan and Bangladesh continue to be married to rich men from oil-rich middle-east countries—against their consent and in defiance of the divine Qur'anic law. In most of these cases, the minors are married to men old enough to be their grandfathers. Invariably, these poor young girls are ditched after a day or two. This practice is still prevalent despite the efforts of an Islamic oversight board in India (the Wakf Board) that has powers to expel Muslim clerics sanctioning such marriages.[147]

Men who support polygamy state, "Women urge the husbands to get second wives so that they do not feel lonely." Perhaps the husbands who support polygamy ought to give their wives some options. What would the wives prefer: for the husbands to get a second wife, or the privilege to visit their friends unescorted during the day while the husbands were at work? Or perhaps would they prefer to take a job or have a helping hand with the household chores, or get marriage counseling to make their conjugal relationship more meaningful? Or would they prefer not to bear any more children?

If these women had options, how many of these housebound wives, some of who may have had genital mutilation [and never experienced sexual gratification], grant permission to their husbands to get other wives?

---

[147]"Uniform Civil Code of India." *Wikipedia, The Free Encyclopedia.* Wikipedia, The Free Encyclopedia, 28 Jun. 2010. Web. 16 July 2010. http://en.wikipedia.org/wiki/Uniform_civil_code_of_India

Muslim women have started challenging the patriarchal marriage laws imposed by the religious leaders. In March 2008, the All India Muslim Women Personal Law Board drafted its own version of marriage laws (*Shariat Nikahnama*) that addressed the fair treatment of women in marriage and divorce.[148] But unfortunately, their version is not enforceable.

The Qur'an has no laws restricting travel by women. And yet, many Islamic nations do not allow women to travel alone. In Afghanistan under the Taliban, and in Saudi Arabia, they are not privileged to drive according to the *Fatwas* (religious rulings).[149] These rules, forced upon the women by the male clerics in order to oppress women, have nothing to do with Islam.

The Qur'an clearly states, "Do not kill a soul made by Allah, except through the due process of law." And, yet, when the male members of the family suspect that a female member of their family is unchaste and her actions will bring dishonor, she is murdered. Sometimes innocent women are stoned to death. While no law is clearly defined in the Qur'an, such honor killings by family are perfectly legal in many Islamic nations.[150]

---

[148]Virendra Nath Bhatt, "Muslim Women Challenge Patriarchal Marriage Code ." OneWorld.Net–17 Mar. 2008. Web. 21Aug. 2010.
http://southasia.oneworld.net/Article/muslim-women-challenge-patriarchal-marriage-code

[149]"Fatwā." *Wikipedia, The Free Encyclopedia.* Wikipedia, The Free Encyclopedia, 7 July 2010. Web. 16 July 2010.
http://en.wikipedia.org/wiki/FatwpercentC4percent81

[150]"Honor Killing." *Wikipedia, The Free Encyclopedia.* Wikipedia, The Free Encyclopedia, 16 July 2010. Web. 16 July 2010.
http://en.wikipedia.org/wiki/Honor_killing

TOLERANCE AND PROSELYTIZING: Non-Muslims once faced discrimination in certain Islamic nations. These non-Muslims were called *Dhimmis*.[151] This status, originally created for the Jews and Christians, was later imposed on other non-Muslim communities. There are examples of restrictions and persecution of Dhimmis throughout history. For example, the Zoroastrians in Seventh Century Persia, the Christians and Jews in Eighth Century Spain during the rule of Moors and Arabs, the Hindus and Buddhists in India and Afghanistan during the Sixteenth Century Mughal rule (Muslim invaders from Persia), the Christians and Jews in the Eighteenth and Nineteenth century Ottoman Empire, and the Mandeans as recently as Nineteenth century Iraq. These discriminatory practices against the *Dhimmis* were imposed after the Pact of Umar (717 CE) and are clearly in defiance of Qur'anic law. *Dhimmis* could not worship in public or display their religious symbols on churches, temples, or synagogues, and could not ring temple or church bells, or could not renovate or re-build their places of worship. They faced either forced conversions to Islam or death; in courts, they could not bear witness against a Muslim; they were enslaved to become soldiers in the slave armies of the Muslim rulers; and were forced to wear special outfits so that they could be easily identified. The *Dhimmis* were not

---

[151]"Dhimmi." *Wikipedia, The Free Encyclopedia*. Wikipedia, The Free Encyclopedia, 16 July 2010. Web. 16 July 2010.
http://en.wikipedia.org/wiki/Dhimmi

allowed to ride horses or camels, but were forced to walk or were restricted to riding only donkeys; they could not build homes higher than Muslim homes; marriage between a *Dhimmi* and Muslim was banned. And they were considered "unclean" and proclaimed so as recently as in Twentieth Century Iran, by Ayatollah Ruhollah Khomeini. Could this be a form of untouchability in Islam?

The Holy Qur'an clearly states, "There should not be coercion in the matter of faith" (Al-Baqarah 2:256). Further, it forbids killing of wounded persons, old persons, children or women. It also forbids "killing monks in monasteries" as well as "people in places of worship." Then how did the highly educated Muslims come to believe that Islam is the only true religion in the eyes of God, and that the other religions and their forms of worship are wrong? Are there any moderate Muslims who can speak up against such ungodly and un-Qur'anic rhetoric in their midst? Or, are they afraid to do so?

One has to wonder who sanctioned the mutilation of statues in temples in India during Mughal rule. And, more recently in 2001, who sanctioned the destruction of the Giant Buddha statue in Bamyan, Afghanistan?[152]

The Qur'an also forbids disgracing and mutilating the corpses of their enemies. And yet, hostages captured by Islamists are killed without a fair trial or hearing, and their bodies are disgraced in public. The perpetrators are seldom brought to

---

[152]"Buddhas of Bamyan." *Wikipedia, The Free Encyclopedia.* Wikipedia, The Free Encyclopedia, 6 July 2010. Web. 16 July 2010.
http://en.wikipedia.org/wiki/Buddhas_of_Bamyan

trial. In fact, they are glorified as jihadists. What should be the punishment of such violators of the Holy law? Why are the clerics silent about such transgressions? Does keeping silent suit their goals of acquiring or staying in power? On what basis can they claim moral high ground?

LEADERSHIP AND ABUSE OF POWER: The Holy Qur'an states that Muslim communities should conduct their business through consultations [*Shura*]. But seldom does real consultation occur. And it is quite common to hear about *fatwa* [religious rulings] handed down by the influential *muftis* (clerics).[153]

In a diverse country such as India, a *fatwa* from one part of India may not be applicable in another. Fortunately, unlike in rigidly Islamic countries, the *fatwas* are treated as advice and not dictum by the practicing Muslims in a secular country like India. Today, quite a few Indian Muslims believe that they did not have enough courage to speak out and reform some of their religious laws at the time of independence when the country's secular laws were being formulated in 1947.[154] Anyway, the question arises whether women are consulted before the declaration of a *fatwa* that directly affects their lives. If

---

[153]Dr. Saddiq A. Abu Al-Hasan, "The Islamic Shura (Consultation) and Modern Democracy," *J of Sharia and Islamic studies*. Kuwait University. Web. 20 Oct 2010.
http://www.kjse.kuniv.edu.kw/jsis/english/showarticle.asp?id=500

[154]Rakhi Chakrabarty, *Everyone Loves a Bad Fatwa*. Mobile e-paper. Bennett Coleman. 2010. Web, 20 July 2010. http://mobilepaper.timesof india.com/mobile.aspx?article=yes&page id=20&sectid=edid=&edlabel= TOIBG&mydateHid=23-05-2010& pubname=Times+of+India+- +Bangalore&edname=&articleid= Ar02000&publabel=TOI

women cannot attend services at mosques and participate in consultations, then how can they possibly have a say in the community? Muslim women who believe that their Sharia law leaves them at a disadvantage cannot do anything to effect change. At least not as long as the male-dominated Muslim boards make all the decisions, among them being the privilege to have multiple wives. It should not come as a surprise that women in India have started to form their own mosques, perhaps to start consultations amongst themselves and apply the divine Qur'anic laws in their communities.[155] Fortunately, there is a also a trend towards allowing women to attend select prayers at some mosques in India.

Judaism

MALE DOMINANCE: The holy book of Judaism, the Torah, including the Ten Commandments, was authored by Moses during His Divine revelation.[156] And according to some scholars, it was authored in part by the Patriarchs. This "Mosaic" authorship of the Torah is now widely accepted, spanning many centuries before being completed in 5 CE. So, the Torah contains the "revealed" and the "rabbinical" commandments—all authored by men. No mention of women's contribution to its authorship is evident. Throughout the Torah, God is clearly

---

[155]Soutik Biswas, "Storm Over Indian Women's Mosque." *BBC.* BBC News Online, 27 Jan. 2004. Web. 17 July 2010.
http://news.bbc.co.uk/2/hi/south_asia/3429695.stm

[156]"Torah." *Wikipedia, The Free Encyclopedia.* Wikipedia, The Free Encyclopedia, 12 July 2010. Web. 17 July 2010.
http://en.wikipedia.org/wiki/Torah

assigned the male gender—The *Lord* is the God, Who created us." [Emphasis added.] Nevertheless, it is remarkable that there are indeed Jewish women who enjoy the title of prophetess— Miriam and Huldah, for example.

In *Haredi* (Orthodox) Judaism, practiced by Hassidic Jews, women are not privileged to be a part of the congregation. They are not considered members of the "public community," but belong only to the domestic realm.[157,158] While some congregations of Modern Orthodox Judaism are allowing women to attend services, they are not privileged to read the Torah. This is done to preserve *Kavod Hatzibur*—"the dignity of the congregation." Because some believe women's participation "harms the sacredness of the synagogue." Recently, and largely due to the efforts of the Jewish Orthodox Feminist Alliance (JOFA), some of the strict rules of the services at the congregation have begun to ease.[159] Consequently, there are mixed prayer groups called Partnership Minyanim, where women are "called upon" by the men to conduct "parts" of the services.[160] Recently, in 2008, a guide to the conduct of Partnership Minyanim was published in *The Jerusalem Post*, much to the

---

[157]"Haredi Judaism." *Wikipedia, The Free Encyclopedia*. Wikipedia, The Free Encyclopedia, 14 July 2010. Web. 17 July 2010.
http://en.wikipedia.org/wiki/Haredi_Judaism

[158]"Women in Judaism." *Wikipedia, The Free Encyclopedia*. Wikipedia, The Free Encyclopedia, 15 July 2010. Web. 17 July 2010.
http://en.wikipedia.org/wiki/Women_in_Judaism

[159]Jewish Orthodox Feminist Alliance. New York. http://www.jofa.org/

[160]"Partnership Minyan." *Wikipedia, The Free Encyclopedia*. Wikipedia, The Free Encyclopedia, 28 Jun. 2010. Web. 17 July 2010.
http://en.wikipedia.org/wiki/Partnership_minyan

chagrin of some orthodox rabbis.[161] Its practice is growing in popularity among the younger and highly educated Jews. This is clearly an indication that the religion is evolving and progressing with the times.

According to ancient Jewish tradition, women were not privileged to learn the Torah and other religious scriptures. However, only the last few decades have seen a reversal of that tradition, and growing numbers of women are now permitted to learn the scriptures.

The Reform movement in Judaism (called Liberal or Progressive in many countries) originated in Germany.[162] As a result, mixed seating and equal participation in synagogues is allowed. However, the social justice and equality falls short in some ways. For example, the first-born son enjoys a special privilege and his birth is celebrated by a special ceremony (*Pidyon Ha-Ben*). The birth of daughters, on the other hand, is not celebrated. The modern Conservative movement is encouraging the celebration of newborn girls by special ceremonies called *Simchat Bat*. There is a special ritual, *Brit Milah*, the naming ceremony of boys when they are given their Hebrew names. (The boys are also circumcised at this time). A similar naming ceremony for girls, *Zevet Habat*, is not so widespread.

---

[161]Michal Lando, "First Guide for Inclusive Prayer Services is Published." J Post. Jerusalem Post Online, 19 Feb. 2008. Web. 17 July 2010. http://www.jpost.com/JewishWorld/JewishNews/Article.aspx?id=92578

[162]"Reform Judaism." *Wikipedia, The Free Encyclopedia*. Wikipedia, The Free Encyclopedia, 14 Jun. 2010. Web. 17 July 2010. http://en.wikipedia.org/wiki/Reform_Judaism

What is the plight of women in Haredi Judaism? In its most benign form there are separate codes of headdresses for men and women. Married women have to cover their hair completely, especially while attending services in synagogues.[163] The men, on the other hand, only wear the *yarmulke*. But the plight of women is rather discouraging in some respects. For example, according to a Biblical law, a woman is left in a dire predicament for her entire life when it pertains to rape. It states in Deuteronomy: 22–28: "If a man find a damsel that is a virgin, which is not betrothed, and lay hold on her, and lie with her, and *they be found in the act*; [emphasis added] then the man that lay with her shall give unto the damsel's father fifty shekels of silver, and she shall be his wife; because he hath humbled her, he may not put her away all his days."[164] Imagine what it must be like for the woman to spend the rest of her life serving and sleeping with her rapist. Furthermore, this "punishment" to the rapist is meted only if "they be found."

WIDOWHOOD: The plight of widows, according to the scriptures, is also less than desirable: Genesis 38:8 states: "And Judah said unto Onan, 'Go in unto thy brother's [widow], and marry her,

---

[163]"Kippah." *Wikipedia, The Free Encyclopedia*. Wikipedia, The Free Encyclopedia, 17 July 2010. Web. 17 July 2010.
http://en.wikipedia.org/wiki/Kippah

[164]King James Version. Deut. 22. 28-29. *Bible Gateway*. Bible Gateway, n.d. Web. 23 July 2010. http://www.biblegateway.com/passage/?search=Deuteronomy+22percent3A28-29&version=KJV

and raise up seed to thy brother.'"[165] In other words, if a woman became a widow before giving birth to a son, she was forced to marry the deceased husband's brother(s) so that the dead brother could have a male heir. Brothers-in-law of widows used this privileged position to coerce the widows into submission (much like the Hindu custom). In such instances, there was no hope for a widow—no matter how young—remarrying anyone else. Furthermore, the Biblical scriptures forbade the priests from officiating the marriages of *widows, divorced women, or prostitutes* (Leviticus 21:13–15). Even today, the *Cohens* (the high priests) of the Jewish faith cannot bless the marriage of any of these unfortunate women. In sharp contrast, a man is privileged to be married again at any time.

TOLERANCE AND PROSELYTIZING: Tolerance of other faiths was discouraged according to the scriptures. They state: "Ye shall utterly destroy all the places, wherein the nations which ye shall possess served their gods, upon the high mountains, and upon the hills, and under every green tree. And ye shall overthrow their altars, and break their pillars, and burn their groves with fire; and ye shall hew down the graven images of their gods, and destroy the names of them out of that place."[166] Do the religious scholars learn this from the scriptures and promote such intolerance? One can only hope that they do not.

---

[165]King James Version. Gen. 38. 8-10. *Bible Gateway*. Bible Gateway, n.d. Web. 23 July 2010. http://www.biblegateway.com/passage/?search=Genesis+38percent3A8-10&version=KJV

[166]King James Version. Deuteronomy 12:2. *Bible Gateway*. Bible Gateway, n.d. Web. 23 July 2010. http://www.kingjamesbibleonline.org/book.php?book=Deuteronomy&chapter=12&verse=2[1]

LEADERSHIP AND ABUSE OF POWER: Even though there is no central world authority in Judaism, the Hassidic Jews of the orthodox sect have a supreme religious leader, called *Rebbe*. The privilege of becoming a *Rebbe* belongs only to the men. The practice is dynastic—the role of the *Rebbe* is patrilineal, *inherited* by males only, regardless of the individual's knowledge of the scriptures, commitment to the task, or conduct. In most of their synagogues, a hierarchy of sorts exists in the conduct of services: the priest (*Cohen*) is the first to initiate the services. He is the direct patrilineal descendant of Aaron, the brother of Moses.[167] Next in the service comes the Levite—another patrilineal descendant of the son of Jacob.[168]

A rabbi, who is an ordained scholar of the scriptures, is in charge of conducting the services of the congregation.[169] In the absence of a rabbi, services can only be conducted by male substitutes, called *Shatz*. The Jewish codes are not explicit about banning women from becoming rabbis. Although, historically, only men were ordained rabbis. The first duly ordained

---

[167]"Kohen." *Wikipedia, The Free Encyclopedia*. Wikipedia, The Free Encyclopedia, 17 July 2010. Web. 17 July 2010.
http://en.wikipedia.org/wiki/Kohen

[168]"Levi." *Wikipedia, The Free Encyclopedia*. Wikipedia, The Free Encyclopedia, 7 July 2010. Web. 17 July 2010. http://en.wikipedia.org/wiki/Levi
Tracey R. Rich, "Rabbis, Priests, and Other Religious Functionaries." *Judaism 101*. Judaism 101, 1995-2001. Web. 17 July 2010.
http://www.jewfaq.org/rabbi.htm

[169]Tracey R. Rich, "Rabbis, Priests, and Other Religious Functionaries." *Judaism 101*. Judaism 101, 1995-2001. Web. 17 July 2010. http://www.jewfaq.org/rabbi.htm

female rabbi was in 1935 Germany. Since then, Reform Judaism has ordained a little over 500 women.[170]

The rabbis abused their status in the community just as Catholic priests did. Women became victims of sexual harassment. And, just as in the Catholic Church, the rabbis also got away without repercussions.[171] According to rabbinical rules, a rabbi could not stand trial—at least not based on the testimony of women. The accused rabbis were either asked to leave or were re-located. Only in 1996 did a rabbi get expelled from the Rabbinical Council of America (RCA) for alleged sexual harassment of women.

☐ ☐ ☐

From the above brief presentation of the world's major organized religions it becomes obvious that by and large they are designed to subjugate women, exclude them from becoming religious scholars and deny them the privilege of contributing to the community outside the domestic realm. What is more disturbing is that the leaders of all the major religions are focused on the ancient written rules of their holy books, interpreting them and imposing them on the believers in modern times. Emphasis is laid on compliance, and not on faith and spirituality. The importance of seeking the Divine seems to be

---

[170]"Rabbi." *Wikipedia, The Free Encyclopedia*. Wikipedia, The Free Encyclopedia, 16 July 2010. Web. 17 July 2010. http://en.wikipedia.org/wiki/Rabbi

[171]Cybe. "Long List of Jewish Child Molester [sic] Rabbis Gets no Media Coverage and Jewish Homosexual Pedophiles are Undisturbed." *100777*, 20 Sept. 2003. Web. 17 July 2010. http://100777.com/node/463

lost somewhere in translation. Wouldn't the whole world be better served through the attainment of a higher level of consciousness so that peace, love and harmony could prevail?

Lighthouses are more helpful than churches.

— Benjamin Franklin (1706–1790)
American statesman, author, and scientist
Actively involved in the framing of the
Declaration of Independence

Men never do evil so completely and cheerfully as when they do it from religious conviction.

— Blaise Pascal (1623–1662)
French Mathematician and physicist

I always distrust people who know so much about what God wants them to do to their fellows.

— Susan B. Anthony (1820–1906)
American women's suffrage leader

When it is a question of money, everybody is of the same religion.

— Voltaire (1694–1778)
French writer and philosopher

Chapter 6
Power and Privilege in Healthcare

The health of the people is really the foundation upon which all their happiness and all their powers as a state depend.

– Benjamin Disraeli (1809–1881)
British statesman and twice Prime Minister

Healthcare is an essential service offered by society. And vast majority of physicians and nurses is truly benevolent. They go beyond the call of duty to care for the sick, often risking their own mental and physical well-being. But the delivery of care, especially in free market economies such as the U.S., it is treated like a commodity, much to the chagrin of patients and care-givers alike. It is driven by bottom-line profits and has a corporate culture like any other industry. What is wrong with that? People who argue in defense of this culture believe that healthcare ought to be treated like any other consumer service and have a price tag commensurate with the services rendered. But stop and consider the funding of care. It is largely paid for by money collected through taxes or through insurance premiums. Therefore, society ought not to treat it like any other commodity. Furthermore, medical education is heavily subsidized by the state or charitable organizations. In other words, if money from taxes, charity or insurance premiums is spent on this essential service, is it fair to apply free market principles in the delivery of healthcare or extend preferential treatment to certain privileged members of society?

Unfortunately, healthcare is treated like any other business, and access to quality healthcare is largely determined by one's privileged status in society. The privileged and powerful can get the best care on demand in the best facilities, bypassing waiting lists and other standards of care in any given system. Caregivers, often find themselves bending the rules to care for the powerful and privileged.

Below is an excerpt from the same open letter mentioned in Chapter 4. It was addressed to the leader of academic medicine, and authored by 20 leading physicians and medical researchers from five continents:[172]

> *The shocking – and growing – gap between the world's rich and the world's poor must not continue. We imagined a future where academic medicine takes the lead in closing this gap.*

Medical schools could easily narrow the gap in healthcare between rich and poor countries. Schools from rich countries partnering with schools from poor countries could pave the way in achieving this goal. Such cooperation would result in improved medical education and the delivery of quality

---

[172]John P A Ioannidis, et al. Open Letter to the Leader of Academic Medicine – *BMJ* 2007; 334: 191-193. Web. 20 July 2010.
http://www.bmj.com/cgi/content/full/334/7586/191

healthcare worldwide. But elitism and rivalries among medical schools *within one* country prevent them from collaborating with each other. One glaring example in the U.S. is the schism between the two medical school systems that grant different degrees: the Doctor of Osteopathy (DO) and the Doctor of Medicine (MD). Students from these two school systems use practically the same books and pass the same national certifying examinations, yet the schools maintain an uncomfortable, elitist distance that is almost ridiculous. So, can the schools in poor foreign countries hope to see any collaboration with the rich nations?

Inequities of care

Approximately 10 million children under the age of five die each year.[173] Ten thousand babies die *every day* within the first month of life, with an equal number born dead. According to the World Health Organization's (WHO) 1990 Global Burden of Disease (GBD) project, children bear *more than half* of the disease burden in low-income countries, with under-nourishment as the cause of death for at least 30 percent of children under the age of five. Almost all the children who survive the postnatal period have preventable and treatable medical conditions.

The WHO is working with governments and private contributors worldwide to deliver integrated and effective care to reduce child deaths. But what are the chances in this adultcentrist and male-dominated world that these voiceless infants and children will have access to skilled medical care? These children are

---

[173]Fact Sheets. *WHO.* World Health Organization, 2010. Web. 17 July 2010. http://www.who.int/mediacentre/factsheets/en/].

helpless victims. Does it not behoove the parents of the children, fathers and mothers alike, to take full responsibility for the upbringing of their children, including their medical care, rather than expect charitable organizations such as the UN to bear the burden? The problem of lack of healthcare for these helpless children is an extension of irresponsible adultcentrist behavior. Perhaps it may be prudent to allow the women to practice birth control instead of bringing children into this world, only to have them die of negligence before they even learn to walk. Which is morally superior, birth control or allowing children to die premature deaths? Isn't the latter tantamount to murder?

Based on the WHO fact sheet, combined maternal and perinatal deaths add up to 6.3 million deaths *each year*. (To put things in perspective: approximately six million Jews were exterminated by the Nazis in Europe over a six-year span during World War II.)[174] One indicator of safety of pregnancy and childbirth used by the public health experts, including the WHO, is the "maternal mortality ratio" (MMR). It is the ratio of number of maternal deaths per *live* births. A high MMR is considered bad and believed to be related to the lack of skilled prenatal and postnatal care. But is mortality from abortions, and the morbidity from abortions and childbirth not relevant to maternal health? Furthermore, an estimated three million babies are stillborn. Shouldn't their numbers also be a good indicator of prenatal care? Complications during pregnancy account for an alarming 15 percent of the deaths of women of

---

[174]"Estimated Number of Jews Killed in the Final Solution." *Jewish Virtual Library.* Web. 20 July 2010.
http://www.jewishvirtuallibrary.org/jsource/Holocaust/killedtable.html

reproductive age worldwide. Most of these are preventable deaths. Additionally, 20 million women suffer illness *after* childbirth that is directly related to the pregnancy. The morbidity and mortality faced by women have a detrimental effect on the well-being of the entire family. Would it not make more sense to assess the delivery of care by indicators that include all the health problems—morbidity and mortality—stemming from pregnancy?

The risk of maternal death is disproportionately high in developing countries. A woman's lifetime risk of maternal death is 1 in 7,300 in developed countries versus 1 in 75 in developing countries. In Niger, which has the highest maternal mortality, a shocking 1 in 7 women die from pregnancy-related causes. This is the failure of the health officials in developing countries. Who are the decision makers allocating funds for prenatal and postnatal care?

The WHO fact sheet reports that teenage pregnancies account for 16 million live births each year. Approximately 10 percent of these or 1.6 million, result from *coerced* sex. Teenage pregnancies are a reflection of the prevailing cultures. They account for 2 percent of the total in China, 18 percent in Latin America and the Caribbean, and greater than 50 percent in sub-Saharan Africa. The majority of these pregnancies, especially those outside Asia, are to unwed teens. Little effort is made to track down the male partners and hold them accountable for the expenses of prenatal and postnatal care *and* raising the child. The young mothers and their children are powerless and bear the entire socioeconomic burden and stigma of this problem. No common or civil laws exist, to date, to address this menacing and pervasive societal problem. Of course, religious leaders would be quick to confine the teens to their homes as a solution. The irresponsible behavior of men in society is entirely glossed over. The WHO Millennium Development Goal 5 to improve maternal health cannot succeed as long as this basic factor is ignored.[175]

In the U.S., the burden of family planning rests almost exclusively on women. Among the family planning surgical interventions available, over 95 percent were performed on women, and less than 5 percent on men, even though the procedures are riskier for women. Furthermore, the cost of tubal ligation is five times that of a vasectomy.[176] Do the (mostly men) policy makers in the health-care industry really care about cutting costs of healthcare?

Inequities in healthcare are also the result of male dominance in the healthcare industry. For example, there are more male than female physicians in the U.S. Consequently, medical research and the delivery of care are gender biased. Recent reports suggest that women are underrepresented in research studies.[177] Moreover, the

---

[175]"Millennium Development Goals: Progress Towards the Health-related Millennium Development Goals." Fact Sheet #290 WHO. World Health Organization, May 2010. Web. 17 July 2010
http://www.who.int/mediacentre/factsheets/fs290/en/index.html

[176]"How Much Does vasectomy Cost?" *Vasectomy.* Web. 20 July 2010.
http://www.vasectomy.com/ArticleDetail.asp?siteid=V&ArticleId=10

[177]Anna C. Mastroianni, Ruth Faden, and Daniel Federman, eds., *Women and Health Research: Ethical and Legal Issues of Including Women in Clinical Studies.* Vol. 2. (Washington, DC: National Academy, 1994) *National Academies*
http://www.nap.edu/openbook.php?record_id=2343&page=1????.

medical problems of women are often assigned to psychological causes. Consequently, female patients are twice as likely to get mood-altering drugs as compared to male patients with similar complaints. [178,179]

Measurements of indirect costs of illness also tend to be male-oriented—based on the amount of lost *earnings*. It matters little what stay-at-home mothers may face or spend on daycare for a visit to the doctor or during hospitalization. Stay-at-home fathers are a still a small minority.

In the U.S., despite state-funded care for the elderly (Medicare), medical care is not as readily provided to these older adults due to age bias harbored by the caregivers [adultcentrism]. Consequently, young caregivers fail to see reversible elements in their elderly patients' complaints. Elderly women are particularly disadvantaged. One common example of denied care is the treatment for breast cancer in women over the age of 70 years.

Greater emphasis on male patients is also evident at the military Veterans Administration (VA) facilities in the U.S. Despite an increasing number of female veterans, women veterans receive less preventive care (such as breast examinations, pelvic examinations and Pap smears), have no outpatient access and

[178]"Study Reveals Underrepresentation of Women in Cardiovascular Studies." *Medical News.* News-Medical, 20 Feb. 2101. Web. 17 July 2010.
http://www.news-medical.nct/news/20100220/Study-reveals-underrepresentation-of-women-in-cardiovascular-clinical-trials.aspx

[179]"Women Underrepresented in Most Cancer Research." *EurekAlert.* EurekAlert, 8 June 2009. Web. 17 July 2010.
http://www.eurekalert.org/pub_releases/2009-06/acs-wui060309.php

have no psychiatric programs at many of the care facilities. Charlotte Muller summarized it well in her book, *Healthcare and Gender* by stating: "The market does not work well for consumers when the basis of the demand is *dependence*. . . . The demand of the economically disempowered and disenfranchised is a weak force for influencing provider and system behavior."[180]

Ethnic minorities are also less likely to get needed healthcare in the U.S. The same holds for developed nations that have minority ethnic and indigenous populations. Based on the report by the U.S. Institute of Medicine in 2003, disparities of care exist because of a number of causes including (1) access barriers (language, geography, and cultural differences; (2) time constraints and pressure for cost containment, i.e., limits on time spent on patients with no allowance for extra time required in translating; and (3) biases harbored by the healthcare provider leading to stereotyping.[181]

The ethnic disparity in healthcare is also partly the direct result of under-representation of the ethnic minorities in the healthcare workforce. According to the 2004 Sullivan Commission on Diversity in Health Workforce in the U.S., non-whites make up over 25 percent of the population, but represent less than nine percent of nurses and less than six percent of physicians.

---

[180]Charlotte Muller, "*Healthcare and Gender.*" Russell Sage Foundation 1992. Print.

[181]"Select Populations and Health Disparities." *IOM.* Institute of Medicine of the National Academies, 2010. Web. 17 July 2010. http://www.iom.edu/Global/Topics/Select-Populations-Health-Disparities.aspx

Are there barriers to entry into the healthcare industry for ethnic minorities? Or is the under-representation due to "lack of aptitude" or the indirect result of the poor quality of their education? If so, whose failing is it?

The 2008 data from the U.S. National Center for Health statistics has shown that mortality differences between blacks and whites in the U.S. still persists where the death rate is 1.3 times greater for the black population than white (i.e., 30 percent greater risk). Also, infant mortality rate is 2.4 times greater, and maternal mortality rate is 3.3 times greater. The use of high-tech interventions in non-whites is less than in whites, even when all clinical indicators such as severity, age, co-morbidities, etc., are identical.[182] These data show that those less privileged have limited access to care and utilization. Such a hierarchy of care is based on bias and stereotyping by healthcare providers regardless of the site—be it a private or public facility, a teaching or non-teaching hospital. This is despite Title VI of the 1964 Civil Rights Act (CRA) that protects persons from discrimination based on race, color and national origin in facilities that receive Federal funds.

Mistrust of the medical establishment in the U.S. is surprisingly common among ethnic minorities, based on personal experience of individuals and the historical records. The most notable recorded example of the abuse of power in healthcare continued well past the passage of the 1964 Title VI of the

---

[182]P.F. Adams, et al. *Summary Health Statistics for the U.S. Population: National Health Interview Survey 2008.* Vital health Statistics series 10, #243. Dec. 2009. Web. 20 July 2010. http://www.cdc.gov/nchs/data/series/sr_10/sr10_243.pdf

CRA.[183] It was a prospective study of African American syphilis patients conducted by the U.S. Public Health Service, to investigate the mortality of untreated disease. The study was continued for almost *two decades after* the availability of penicillin in 1947. The U.S. Center for Disease Control (CDC) and Prevention, as well as the American Medical Association (AMA), supported the continuation of the study till 1969, five years *after* the passage of Title VI of CRA in 1964. Had there been a fair representation of blacks at the CDC and the AMA, perhaps the lives of countless blacks may have been saved with the use of penicillin. It wasn't until 1972 that the study finally ended. How can one justify such decisions and actions of those in positions of authority? In 1997, President Clinton issued an apology to the research participants and their families and offered reparations.

Recently, increased efforts are being made to provide culturally sensitive healthcare to minorities by ethnically diverse providers. A shift from an ethnocentric to an ethno-relativistic mindset is encouraged. What a refreshing departure from the rigidly judgmental and biased past.[184]

---

[183]"Tuskegee Syphilis Experiment." *Wikipedia, The Free Encyclopedia.* Wikipedia, The Free Encyclopedia, 3 July 2010. Web. 17 July 2010. http://en.wikipedia.org/wiki/Tuskegee_syphilis_experiment

[184]Geri-Ann Galanti, Ph.D. *Caring for Patients from Different Cultures* and *Cultural Sensitivity: A Pocket Guide for Healthcare Professional.* Web. 20 July 2010. *http://resources.performax3.com/releases/documents/ The_Cultural_Competence_inpercent20Health_Care_Series_2.09.pdf*

Socioeconomic disparities and access to healthcare are often brushed aside by blaming the victim, a mindset that usually is a manifestation of irrational xenophobia. Enculturation of citizen groups (i.e., those who maintain their cultural identity) is perceived by the majority caregivers as un-patriotic. And communication barriers that arise in such situations are used as an excuse for extending inferior quality care. The result of such an attitude is poor health outcomes.

Below are some examples of poor care to ethnic minorities:[185]

◊ African American women are twice as likely to die of cervical cancer than white women.

◊ Death rate from heart diseases is 29 percent higher in African American adults than among white adults.

◊ Death rate from stroke is 40 percent higher in African Americans than among white adults.

◊ A whopping 20 percent of Latino patients go without care due to the language barrier.

It is possible that some of the above differences in outcomes may well be the result of genetic predispositions. But efforts are being made to eliminate inequalities of care due to other factors. In 2008, the Office of Minority Health in the Department of Health and Human Services developed standards for culturally and linguistically appropriate services (CLAS).[186] Additionally,

---

[185]2001 Healthcare Quality Survey, *The Commonwealth Fund*. Web. 20 July 2010. http://www.commonwealthfund.org/Content/Surveys/2001/ 2001-Health-Care-Quality-Survey.aspx

[186]National Standards on Culturally and Linguistically Appropriate Services. HHS. 18 July 2010. Web. http://minorityhealth.hhs.gov/templates/ browse.aspx?lvl=2&lvlID=15

the Joint Commission has made the delivery of CLAS an accreditation requirement for hospitals and clinics. The reason for such efforts is that the *long-term* cost benefits of healthy outcomes in society far outweigh the inconvenience caused to caregivers and the small cost of interpreter services.

Organ Trade

Donating organs is a noble cause. It saves thousands of lives every year and improves the quality of life of people suffering end stage disease. According to the WHO, at least 200,000 people are on the waiting lists for kidney transplants worldwide. Approximately 60,000 kidney transplants are performed every year; they are carried out in 91 member countries. In 2005, 21,000 liver and 6,000 heart transplants were also performed worldwide.[187]

However, do the powerful and the privileged have faster and easier access to organs? Do they often bypass national and international waiting lists, regulations, protocols and policies? Patients desperate to obtain an organ are willing to spend money and travel to foreign countries. Such demand by the privileged rich, and a generous supply of organs from the poor in developing countries, has led to what is commonly called "transplant tourism." A report by Organs Watch, an organization based at the University of California, Berkley, identified Bolivia, Brazil, Colombia, India, Iraq, the Republic

---

[187]"Human Organ and Tissue Transplantation." *WHO*. World Health Organization, 2010. Web. 17 July 2010.
http://www.who.int/ethics/topics/human_transplant/en/

of Moldova, Peru, Turkey and Sub-Saharan African nations as organ exporting countries, while Australia, Canada, Israel, Japan, Oman, Saudi Arabia, and the U.S. are recognized as major organ-importing countries.

Transplant tourism is very lucrative for the transplant centers.[188] It has opened the doors to the commercialization of organ transplantation, leading to unscrupulous practices that result in escalating costs, inequitable allocation of deceased donor organs, fraud, coercion and exploitation of living donors. The official WHO figures suggest that roughly 6,000 transplants involve cash payments to poor donors where postoperative care for them is often woefully lacking. According to official records, the estimated risk of the death of a donor is as high as 1 in 3,000.[189] (To put things in perspective, the worldwide mortality from lung cancer is 1 in 5,000.) The actual mortality and morbidity of organ donors may be considerably higher. Will donors continue to offer their organs to save lives if they are treated so shabbily?

In India, the donors usually come from the poorest rural areas, lured by thugs and transported to the clinics where they receive US $800–1,500 from transplant centers. The recipients are

[188]"Transplant Tourism" Causing International Concern. *The Independent*. The Independent, 26 Mar. 2010. Web. 17 July 2010
http://www.independent.co.uk/life-style/health-and-families/transplant-tourism-causing-international-concern-1928293.html

[189]"WHO Proposes Global Agenda on Transplantation."
WHO. World Health Organization, 30 Mar. 2007. Web. 17 July 2010.
http://www.who.int/mediacentre/news/releases/2007/pr12/en/index.html

usually overseas clients who pay up to US $40,000–160,000 for an organ transplant. Most of the profit goes to the clinic operators and facilitators. Despite a legal ban on organ trade in India, transplant tourism goes on unabated. According to the Voluntary Health Association of India, approximately 2,000 Indians sell a kidney every year—most going to foreigners. Such kidneys are transplanted into the more privileged clients who usually hail from the United States, England, Canada, Saudi Arabia and Greece.

In Saudi Arabia, each donor gets cash and other life-long benefits. Nevertheless, the privileged among the Saudis travel abroad to buy organs, bypassing waiting lists at home. Four hundred kidney transplants take place in Saudi Arabia every year, but a greater number, approximately 600, are received abroad.[190] There have also been allegations that embassy officials of certain Middle Eastern countries have facilitated overseas commercial kidney transplants in poor countries such as Pakistan and the Philippines. Is such organ trade not mercenary in the eyes of Islam?

In 1991, the World Health Assembly endorsed the WHO Guiding Principles forbidding organ sales, which state: "The human body and its parts cannot be the subject of commercial transactions. Accordingly, giving or receiving payment (including any other compensation or reward) for organs should be prohibited." Such rhetoric can only be successful if donors are treated with equal respect and compassion.

---

[190]Paul Garwood, "Dilemma Over Live-donor Transplantation." *WHO.* World Health Organization, 2010. Web. 17 July 2010.
http://www.who.int/bulletin/volumes/85/1/07-020107/en/

Under the General Agreement of Trade in Service (GATS), governments of member nations may choose to *trade* health services to achieve their national health objectives. For example, the Philippine government is moving toward institutionalization of paid kidney donations and the acceptance of foreign patients. Are the Filipinos so altruistic? Or, are the policy makers influenced by foreign interests? The privileged foreigners obviously stand to gain from such government policies. It will be interesting to observe what sort of care the poor and powerless Philippine donors will get under this altruistic program.

Organ trade has another sinister aspect. Consent for organ donation is obtained from prisoners on death row. In China, around 12,000 kidney and liver transplants were performed in 2005; most of the transplant organs were allegedly obtained from executed prisoners who had signed the consents while in prison. In a non-democratic country, questions arise as to how many donors may have been incarcerated under false pretext (timed with the arrival of a wealthy client perhaps?), and whether consent was obtained under duress. Most of these organs go to transplant tourists. For example, over half the 900 kidney and liver transplants performed at one major Chinese transplant center in 2004 were on transplant tourists from 19 different countries.[191]

---

[191] *The State of the International Organ Trade: A Provisional Picture Based on Integration of Available Information.* -Yosuke Shimazono in a Bulletin of the WHO. Volume 85: Number 12, Dec. 2007, 901-980. Web. 20 July 2010. http://www.who.int/bulletin/volumes/85/12/06-039370/en/index.html

Here is what the WHO officials have to say about the transplant industry:

◊ *Ethical practices in organ donation and transplantation, as well as access to organs, are of paramount concern. We need to ensure transparency and address legislation appropriately to prevent trade in organs and exploitation of humans.*
  –Dr Samlee Plianbangchang, WHO Regional Director. (Excerpted from an address at the opening of a South-East Asia regional meeting in New Delhi, 2009).

◊ *Transparency should encompass all transplantation organizations, activities, and outcomes, while maintaining the necessary anonymity and privacy of donors and recipients.* –Luc Noël, Department of Essential Health Technologies, World Health Organization, 20 Avenue; Appia, 1211 Geneva 27, Switzerland.

Organized Medicine

Practically every nation has organizations of healthcare providers. The U.S. has the American Medical Association (AMA), American Nurses Association, American Hospitals Association (AHA), etc; the UK has the Royal Colleges of Surgeons and Physicians; India and many other countries have the equivalent of the Medical Council.

Consider the AMA and AHA. The AMA was first formed in 1847 by Nathan Smith Davis in New York. The AMA "helps doctors help patients by *uniting physicians* [emphasis added] nationwide to work on the most important professional and public health issues faced by the nation."[192] The AHA, founded in 1898, "leads, represents and serves hospitals, health systems and other related organizations, and their patients and communities . . . "[193] The emphasis in the stated missions seemed to focus primarily on empowering members of the organizations rather than the patients.

After the September 11 terrorist attacks on select U.S. targets, physicians of the world made an official declaration. It defined the role of physicians in society where the *whole humanity is the patient* [emphasis added]. The nine declarations were duly adopted by the AMA in December 2001.[194] Among them were:

◊ Respect human life and the dignity of every individual

◊ Treat the sick and injured with competence and compassion and without prejudice

◊ Apply our knowledge and skills when needed, though doing so may put us at risk

◊ Advocate for social, economic, educational, and political changes that ameliorate suffering and contribute to human well-being.

---

[192] Our Mission. *AMA*. American Medical Association, 1995-2010. Web. 17 July 2010. http://www.ama-assn.org/ama/pub/about-ama/our-mission.shtml

[193] AHA Mission and Vision. *AHA*. American Hospital Association, 2006-2010. Web. 17 July 2010. http://www.aha.org/aha/about/mission.html

[194] "Declraration of Professional Responsibility," *AMA* Web. 24 Oct 2010. http://www.ama-assn.org/ama1/pub/upload/mm/369/decofprofessional.pdf

Such ideals were woefully needed in the healthcare industry which unfortunately was turning into an ugly, mercenary business. Of course, widespread acceptance of the declarations and a change in the culture will take time.

Meanwhile, despite their good intentions, the AMA [and AHA] seems poorly equipped to address the current crisis of rising costs of healthcare or the delivery of much needed care to the working poor in the U.S. Consequently, American patients are flocking to foreign countries to get essential healthcare. Medical tourism is a booming industry in the countries that provide the much needed care. For example, in 2007, 450,000 foreigners, including Americans, traveled to India for tertiary level care for cardiac, neurological and orthopedic surgeries.[195] Thanks to the efforts of third-party payers and the Joint Commission-International for establishing quality standards at foreign hospitals and clinics. They make affordable and quality care in foreign countries available to those millions who cannot afford the high costs of care at home or the hefty out-of-pocket expenses called co-pays. Do the AMA and AHA look favorably upon medical tourism? It will become evident over time, based on whether they lobby against it or for it.

Currently, it seems as though medical tourism is discouraged. The U.S. government-funded care for the elderly, Medicare, does not pay for care received offshore, even if it means saving

---

[195]Nirmala M Nagaraj, "India Emerges 2nd in Medical Tourism Race." *India Times.* The Times of India, 27 Mar. 2009. Web. 17 July 2010. http://timesofindia.indiatimes.com/india/India-emerges-2nd-in-medical-tourism-race/articleshow/4321310.cms

billions of tax dollars. One has to wonder why, especially in the face of huge budget shortfalls. The Medicare budget for 2009 was $425.5 billion.[196] Those opposed to offshore care argue that it inconveniences the elderly because of the traveling involved. But what if travel was eliminated and certain services were provided over cyberspace, just as it has been provided to countless naval officers? Will healthcare organizations favor and lobby the government to pay for such offshore care? When hundreds of billions of dollars are involved, decisions may not always be in the best interest of the elderly patients. The free market principles are conveniently ignored by the very people who lobby for them when it suits them.

Is it possible that healthcare organizations influence the decisions made by policy makers? Consider this: In the 2008 U.S. presidential election, over 300 healthcare political action committees (PACs) paid over $45 million to various political candidates on both sides of the political aisle, of which healthcare professionals paid over $20 million and pharmaceutical companies paid over $13 million.[197] Given such campaign contributions, who is likely to wield more power in healthcare legislation, the average patient and communities or the powerful organizations with their PAC money?

---

[196]United States. Dept. of Health and Human Services. "HHS Proposes $737 Billion Budget for Fiscal Year 2009." Press Release. HHS, n.d. Web. 17 July 2010.
http://www.hhs.gov/news/press/2008pres/02/20080204a.html

[197]"PAC Contributors to Federal Candidates, 2008." Open Secrets.org. Center for Responsive Politics, 2010. Web. 20 July 2010.
http://www.opensecrets.org/pacs/sector.php?cycle=2008&txt=H01

The U.K. and other Commonwealth countries have a government-funded National Health Service (NHS), with free access to all. However, they also have their share of powerful healthcare organizations.[198]Notable among them are the Royal Colleges of Medical specialists such as the Royal College of Physicians (RCP),[199] and the Royal College of Surgeons (RCS), among others. The Royal Charter was granted to the first of these organizations by Henry VIII in 1518. How do these colleges influence healthcare today? According to the statements on their official website in 2009, the RCP influences healthcare by establishing ". . . priorities for developing policy and influencing government." Further, "the college officers devote their efforts in 'representing *members' interests* [emphasis added],'" and help "support these members through training, events and with excellent value-for-money publications." The RCP mission also states, "We also lead medical debate, and lobby and advise government and other decision makers on behalf of *our members* [emphasis added]." Its "policy and public affairs staff work closely with Government and other stakeholder organizations to promote improvements to patient care."[200]

[198]"About the NHS." *NHS.* National Health Service, 2010. Web. 17 July 2010. http://www.nhs.uk/NHSEngland/thenhs/about/Pages/overview.aspx

[199]"Founding the College." College History. *RCP.* Royal College of Physicians, n.d. Web. 17 July 2010. http://www.rcplondon.ac.uk/history-heritage/College-history-new/Pages/Overview.aspx

[200]"About the College." *RCP.* Royal College of Physicians, n.d. Web. 17 July 2010. http://www.rcplondon.ac.uk/About-the-college/Pages/about.aspx

If such professional organizations protect the interests of their members, it should not come as a surprise that even though the Royal College has been around since 1518, it took more than four centuries to introduce the Patient Involvement Unit (PIU).[201] According to the official website, one of the stated missions of PIU is "Working with the Specialist Societies (i.e., the Royal Colleges of specialists) to find ways of increasing patient and public engagement, involvement and effectiveness." While the PIU was created in September 2003, it had its dedicated administrator only in January 2007. One can only hope that the physicians' organizations may finally heed the powerless patients' concerns.

The U.K.'s NHS boasts free healthcare to all. Meanwhile, the taxpayers pay $180 billion every year (the UK's total defense budget is only $60 million). In other words, it costs every man, woman, and child approximately £1,500 (US$3,000/year or $250/month.)[202] Some might argue that the sum is quite reasonable for free healthcare for all. However, the NHS is plagued by long waiting times and substandard care. In a

[201]"Patient Involvement Unit." *RCP*. Royal College of Physicians, n.d. Web. 17 July 2010. http://www.rcplondon.ac.uk/patients-carers/Pages/Patient-Involvement-Unit.aspx

[202]"The NHS in England." *NHS*. National Health Service, 4 Dec. 2009. Web. 17 July 2010. http://www.nhs.uk/NHSEngland/thenhs/about/Pages/overview.aspx

recent report by CBS reporter Larry Miller, it was pointed out that the system suffers from a "government-imposed culture of 'command and control.'" Since funding is directly related to demand, the regional health authorities create long waiting lists to demand more funding.[203] What is more interesting is that the multi-billion-dollar NHS of the U.K. employs more than 1.7 million people. Of those, only about 850,000 are directly involved in patient care. What do the rest of them do? Perhaps some of them serve as administrators. Whose interests are the power-wielding healthcare administrators and organizations likely to serve——their own or the patients'? It is estimated that 25 percent of NHS hospitals do not even meet the minimum standards for hygiene. Patients get so tired of waiting for their care that some prefer to treat themselves. For example, "a woman pulled seven of her teeth with pliers because she could not find an NHS dentist and could not afford private treatment. Others say they use super glue to secure crowns and bridges for the same reasons."[204]

Another form of abuse that has now become prevalent is in the care of elderly population. For example, in the U.S., perfectly ambulatory older citizens living in independent-living communities are incorrectly labeled "home-bound." At such living facilities, a nurse is assigned to provide care in the same

---

[203, 204]Larry Miller, "Problems With U.K. National Health System." Letter From London. *CBS.* CBS News, 20 Oct. 2007. Web. 17 July 2010.
http://wap.cbsnews.com/site?sid=cbsnews&pid=sections.detail&catId=
TOP&index=0&storyId=3386222&type=null&searchKey=null&viewFull
=yes://www.cbsnews.com/stories/2009/06/27/eveningnews/main
5119109.shtml

building with easy access so that the residents can easily walk to the office. If residents at the facility go to the nurse's office for an adhesive bandage for a minor abrasion, they are asked to return home and the nurse follows to affix the adhesive bandage in the residents' homes. Furthermore, the nurse charges for a few subsequent home visits. These elderly residents are secretly labeled "home-bound" in the system even though they may be perfectly ambulatory and travel to visit doctors on a regular basis.[205] What does this mean to the caregivers and the taxpayers? To the caregivers it is a money making bonanza; each home visit costs $100 [a minor abrasion can cost a total of $500]. To the tax payers it is a huge drain on precious resources. What other forms of abuse of the system exist? The U.S. government spending on healthcare in 2010 topped $ 1.1 trillion, a colossal 17% of the annual budget.[206] The cost to taxpayers for such abusive practices is liable to get worse with the aging baby-boomers.

Could such blatant abuses take place at accredited healthcare facilities and hospitals? Are unnecessary tests or care extended to trusting patients who are least likely to suspect fraud? Are charges falsely inflated? And, if so, what is it costing the taxpayers and those with private insurance? Is it any wonder that the government has enacted laws against such fraud and set up toll-free numbers for whistle-blowers? Citizens

---

[205]Personal communication of a friend.

[206]Christopher Chantrill, "Government Spending Breakdown," *USGovernmentspending.com*. Web. 24 Oct 2010.
http://www.usgovernmentspending.com/breakdown

must become mindful of such abuses and act to curtail them. If every person takes on the responsibility—including those receiving care—the problem may be solved. Americans can call 1-800-447-8477, or write to the office of the Inspector General, Department of Health and Human Services; PO Box 23489, Washington DC 20026.

In India, there was an entrenched culture of incompetence, corruption and cronyism within the Medical Council of India (MCI). The MCI was woefully inept in addressing even the basics such as medical education, standards of care and self-policing. The situation was so bad that the head of the Council was taking bribes to issue certificates to institutions that did not meet the established standards. Consequently, in May 2010, the President of India, the Hon. Ms. Patil, at the request of the Health Secretary, Ms. Sujatha Rao, dissolved the MCI and established a six-member panel of eminent physicians to actively run the affairs of healthcare in the country for a maximum of one year.[207] Meanwhile, a new entity will be created that will be responsible for self-policing and medical education in the country.

In Japan, the national medical insurance system is believed to be one of the best in the world, as it enables anybody to receive medical treatment anywhere, anytime. But even its system is controlled by powerful Japanese physicians and caregivers. One of the ways in which it does so is by allowing only doctors or nurses trained in Japan to practice. Even Japanese trained in the medical profession in Australia or Europe are not allowed

---

[207]Kounteya Sinha, "MCI Dissolved," *TNN/The Hindu*, 16 May 2010. Print.

to return and join the Japanese medical system. The entrenched and powerful medics in the system argue that unless doctors are "familiar with the Japanese language, customs or medical practices, they will not be able to offer effective treatment to Japanese patients." Such restrictions imposed on foreign-trained Japanese doctors by the domestically-trained exist even though hospitals and healthcare centers all across Japan are overwhelmed and refuse to admit new patients because of nurse shortages. [Japan is not an exception in this regard; the scenario is similar in many other countries]. Some hospitals have to turn away outpatients due to a shortage of doctors. The physicians wield so much power that they manage all the hospitals. These physicians are not business savvy; almost 90 percent of university hospitals are in the red and are re-ceiving government subsidies.[208] And if the overworked care-givers make a mistake, they simply apologize. There are no medical malpractice lawsuits; the patients have no recourse.

Sweden, known for its womb-to-tomb social services, also has power brokers in the delivery of healthcare. Since 1955, the national government has given increasing authority and responsibility for the healthcare system to the "county councils." These councils have more power over the healthcare system than the physicians, the patients and both the national or

---

[208]Mukesh Williams, "Can the Japanese Medical System be Revitalized?" *Boloji* Boloji Media, 7 Oct. 2007. Web. 17 July 2010. http://www.boloji.com/opinion/0417.htm.

municipal governments.[209] The county councils deal with the problem of high demand for healthcare by rationing care—by instituting waiting lists for medical appointments and surgery. Patients who do not wish to wait can go to private practitioners. But it is not that straightforward. The powerful county councils also control the private healthcare market by heavily regulating the number of private physicians. Every private physician has to have an agreement with the county council in order to be reimbursed by the government. Furthermore, the councils regulate the number of patients that private providers can see in a year. Are the bureaucrats running the county councils *for* healthcare or *against it*? Is there room for bribery and fraud?

Abuses by Patients

Do patients also abuse healthcare systems? The answer is yes. In most existing systems, certain individuals abuse their privileges as citizens; their irresponsible behavior becomes the financial burden of the responsible members of society. Some glaring examples are the costs of treating irreversible liver damage caused by alcoholism, or emphysema and lung cancer caused by smoking. These irresponsible citizens either expect free care at tax-funded healthcare facilities, or they lie about their dangerous life styles and their addictions when they buy private insurance. Perhaps health education and maintenance ought to be an integral part of healthcare delivery.

[209]David Hogberg, "Sweden's Single-Payer Health System Provides a Warning to Other Nations." *National Policy Analysis*. National Center for Public Policy Research, May 2007. Web. 17 July 17, 2010. http://www.nationalcenter.org/NPA555_Sweden_Health_Care.html

Modern society seems to lay greater emphasis on automobiles and road safety than it does on health [not illness]. Governments in most countries carefully regulate proper driving credentials, and allow only the use of registered and insured vehicles that are subject to regular inspections. In the U.S., the Division of Motor Vehicle (DMV) does just that. The government also ensures safe roads. And it is the responsibility of every citizen to comply *and pay* for the costs involved to abide by the state regulations in order to drive an automobile. So, why isn't health *maintenance* treated the same way? What would happen if traffic systems were treated like the current healthcare systems? There would be frequent vehicular breakdowns and road accidents causing widespread morbidity and mortality. The breakdowns and accidents would clog the over-utilized and crumbling roadways. Isn't this the state of health clinics and hospitals in most countries? Is this inability to deal with the problem a blind spot? Healthcare facilities all over the world are overwhelmed with demand, while the cost of delivery is a rising spiral. Something seems amiss. Or, does the inability result from manipulation by the powerful and well-connected organizations that are directly or indirectly related to the delivery of care to the sick and dying? There is a growing trend in private and public sectors, encouraging health education, maintenance and prevention. However, could those involved with the delivery of care also manipulate such preventative and maintenance programs to further their cause? Shouldn't altruism and compassion be at the core?

To that end, in 2010, the Radiological Society of North America (RSNA) made a public statement on Professionalism which prescribes to its members putting the *interests of patients above those of physicians* [emphasis added]; it also lists essential components of medicine's contract with society that address ethics, honesty with patients, cultural sensitivity, just distribution of finite resources and eliminating conflicts of interest, among other things.[210]

◊ ◊ ◊

Whatever the business model used, compassion and fairness ought to be integral to the delivery of care to the sick and dying, with respect for all, regardless of class, color or creed. Also, the delivery of care should not be driven merely by bottom-line profits or as a one-size-fits-all tax-funded program. And above all, trust must be universal.

It is no measure of health to be well adjusted to a profoundly sick society.

– Jiddu Krishnamurti (1895–1986)

Indian philosopher

---

[210]RSNA Statement on Professionalism. 2010. Web. 24 Oct 2010. http://www.rsna.org/About/professionalism.cfm

Chapter 7
Power and Privilege in the Justice System

The Court is forever adding new stories to the temples of constitutional law, and the temples have a way of collapsing when one story too many is added.
— Justice Robert H. Jackson (1892–1954)

U.S. Attorney General and
Chief prosecutor at Nuremberg trials

Unequal Treatment under the Law

Having money makes all the difference in how justice is delivered. Those so privileged, even if guilty as charged, can either pay bail or hire a lawyer to get out of jail. Meanwhile, people without money, even if innocent, often languish in jails until the court appoints a public defender and the system has time for legal proceedings. Alternatively, these wrong-fully incarcerated innocent people plea bargain for a lesser charge to get out of jail, only to have the crime—which they did not commit—permanently etched in their record.

Thus, the system seems to work in favor of criminals with money. How many innocent people are wrongfully accused and convicted in such a system? Furthermore, could poor people be wrongfully charged to show the average taxpayers that the system is working to keep crime off the streets? Or could innocent people be tried and convicted by the powers that be to meet their quotas for career advancement?

Paralyzed and Clogged Courts

Without lawyers and their expertise, justice would be hard to find in modern society. But criminals seem to enjoy more privileges than the victims of crime. To whom do American citizens owe this discrepancy in the criminal justice system? They owe it largely to the existing legal system. According to an experienced New York State Supreme Court Judge, Hon. Harold J. Rothwax, the foremost question in a criminal case never gets addressed: Did you do it? Do the judges have the power to conduct court proceedings to get to the bottom of the matter and answer that fundamental question? The answer is no. Their power is merely an illusion. Instead of seeking the truth, evidence of wrong doing is sought. And incriminating evidence can only be gathered according to strict regulations. So, even when a criminal case is crystal clear, the criminals with help from their defense lawyers find ways to mask the truth.

So how is evidence suppressed in the legal justice system? One of the ways used is the protection under the Fourth Amendment of the U.S. Constitution,[211] which states, "The right of the people to be secure in their persons, houses, papers, and effects, against unreasonable searches and seizures, shall not be violated, and no warrants shall issue, but upon probable cause . . ." So if any evidence is gathered without all due process and paperwork, it gets thrown out in the courts and

---

[211]"Fourth Amendment to the United States Constitution." *Wikipedia, The Free Encyclopedia*. Wikipedia, The Free Encyclopedia, 13 July 2010. Web. 17 July 2010. http://en.wikipedia.org/wiki/Fourth_Amendment_to_the_United_States_Constitution

cannot be used ever again.[212] The police officers have to be extremely cautious as they proceed with the arrest of a criminal. Is this not a rather misguided interpretation of the Fourth Amendment? It does not suggest anywhere that if incriminating evidence is available it should be thrown out and not be presented in the courts. Clearly, this plays out in favor of the criminals. The victims of crime are powerless.

Furthermore, no criminal can be questioned by the police or any law enforcement officer once he or she has been formally charged of committing a crime. According to the Sixth Amendment of the U.S. Constitution, the suspect or criminal has to have legal counsel present at all interrogations.[213] So confessions or any incriminating statements made to prison guards or police officers can never be presented in court as admission of guilt. Imagine that. A criminal confesses to a law enforcement officer at the scene of the crime, and yet that confession can never be presented in court. Of course, there is a remote possibility that a guard or an officer may coerce the criminals into making incriminating statements. But, does it make any sense to not present it at all in the court? Is it not empowering the criminals? The task of some defense lawyers seems to be the training of the criminals to lie and hide the truth. What is even more disturbing is that repeat offenders

---

[212]Harold J. Rothwax, *Guilty: The Collapse of Criminal Justice* (New York: Random House, 1996). Print.

[213]"Sixth Amendment to the United States Constitution." *Wikipedia, The Free Encyclopedia*. Wikipedia, The Free Encyclopedia, 9 July 2010. Web. 17 July 2010. http://en.wikipedia.org/wiki/Sixth_Amendment_to_the_ United_States_Constitution

who have been indicted and who are out on parole go on committing more crimes and they cannot be questioned about their new crimes without legal counsel. A lot of them go free as a result of this interpretation of the Sixth Amendment. It empowers the repeat offenders—the drug dealers, serial killers and serial rapists.

What other privilege do the criminals enjoy? They enjoy the right to a speedy trial. Clearly, the law was designed to help innocent suspects so that they would not be incarcerated for prolonged periods of time without a trial. But serial offenders, with the help of their defense lawyers, use this loophole quite well. Parolees disappear and conveniently appear on the scene—well past the "speedy trial" deadline. The case gets dismissed because it did not meet the deadline. Some defense lawyers assist and abet in this game played by career criminals—even if the courts are not backlogged with cases. The suspects' guilt is irrelevant and the cases get dismissed no matter how heinous the crimes. One can only imagine the frustration of the judges in such cases. The safety of society is at risk. The defense lawyers who get such criminals off the hook are not accountable for any new crimes committed by their clients. There is no security for the victims.

The U.S. criminal justice system is big business for the defense team because "90 percent of the people who go to trial are guilty." So the defense team has a lot at stake. The system is only about winning the case, not about getting to the truth. One historic case in 1994 involved a double murder in which the case was manipulated most successfully to get the murderer off the hook because the accused was rich and famous. The jury selection took six weeks. The selection process was tedious—the prospective jurors had to fill out an 80 page application that had over 290 questions. Needless to say that, at the trial, evidence was suppressed or manipulated to hide the facts.[214]

Furthermore, the system is marred by conflict of interest that arises because of the system of judge appointments. They are chosen from the ranks of defense lawyers. Could the judges have close friends in the community of lawyers they worked with before their appointment? It makes one wonder. This ineffective legal justice system with "inert" judges and passive juries could be changed overnight by having a separate career line for judges.

Even if judges were not beholden to their lawyer friends, they are fearful of even the slightest misstep that will work in favor of criminals. Cases get dismissed if the smallest mistake is made by the police, the prosecution team or the judge. This occurs so frequently that verdicts are reversed if any one of them makes an error, and the criminals consequently get off scot-free. Imagine how rape victims must feel to see their rapists set free on a technicality. And that is all because the American judges are powerless (unlike their European and Asian counterparts), and play a passive role as listeners only.

Furthermore, the courts are clogged with cases, the judges overworked, and the proceedings too complex. A review of legal

---

[214]Harold J. Rothwax, *Guilty: The Collapse of Criminal Justice* (New York: Random House, 1996). Print.

proceedings in well-publicized cases, often involving the defense of the powerful and the privileged, can be quite revealing.[215]

Do average citizens and victims of crime hope to see justice in the current system? It certainly seems bleak. Only 10 percent of arrests lead to indictments. In other words, approximately 90 percent of the cases are plea-bargained. So the punishment befitting a crime is reduced to a fine and a mere slap on the wrist instead of a jail sentence. This is done not because the judges are lazy, but because the system is inefficient. It is so because there are often ten trial parts, with each court appearance taking hours of negotiations and scheduling.

Judge Rothwax expresses his frustrations with the legal system throughout his book, *Guilty: The Collapse of Criminal Justice.* He believes that power and money help erect screens that hide the truth and that the "American courtroom is dangerously out of order."[216]

The situation is even worse in India.[217] In the late 1990s, a retiring Chief Justice of India was so discouraged by the administration of criminal law that he declared the system "had collapsed." This is mainly because the police are empowered to investigate all criminal cases. As a result, the workload

---

[215, 216] Harold J. Rothwax, *Guilty: The Collapse of Criminal Justice* (New York: Random House, 1996). Print.

[217] Fali S. Nariman – *India's Legal system: Can it be Saved?* (New Delhi: Penguin Books India 2006). Print

of the police is prohibitive. Moreover, they are overworked and underpaid. So, too, are the judges. For example, 1.3 million police handle 5 million crimes registered every year. The number of judges booking criminal cases in the lower courts of the entire country, of over 1 billion, is an appalling 12,000. Consequently, there are over 13 million pending cases. The entire budget for the legal services is a paltry Rs.30 million (or less than U.S. $1 million). Therefore, only 19 percent of criminal cases are tried each year. Furthermore, the police are stretched so thin that people neither trust nor expect the police to investigate cases fairly.

Worse still, the accused are sometimes tortured by the inept police and innocents are forced to admit to crimes they never committed. Some cases even get fast-tracked to bring undeserved glory to the officers for their promotion. The cases are handled so poorly that less than 45 percent of the tried criminals get convicted. [In contrast, the rate of convictions is over 90 percent in the U.K., France and Japan]. The law-abiding citizens are powerless. There has been talk—only talk—of establishing a separate forensic investigative team so that criminal cases are handled more efficiently. Such an alternative would also free up police to actually provide surveillance in the neighborhoods and provide invaluable service to the citizens of India.

In the mid 1990s, the situation was more dismal in the handling of civil cases in India. As a result of the backlog of cases, it took several *decades* to resolve issues. Bribes were commonplace. Indians dreaded the courts. Finally, in the mid-1900s, with the help of the Chief Justices of High Courts and judges of the Supreme Court of India, pending civil cases, such as motor accident cases, were settled in *Lok Adalats*—literally meaning "courts of the people." In these courts, disputes are now *settled* by the consent of the parties involved. From 1996 to 2005, such people's courts have increased in number from 13,000 to over 450,000 and the number of cases handled rose from roughly 300,000 to over 1.7 million. The courts are conducted by retired justices.

Misconduct

A few judges behave in inappropriate ways. According to Professor Marina Angel of Temple University School of Law, "[Some] Judges have solicited sexual favors from criminals, defendants, civil litigants, lawyers, law clerks, law students, court employees, job applicants, probation officers, juvenile court wards and jurors."[218] Seldom are judges removed from the bench for such misconduct. Even in cases of statutory rape of minors, the only thing the judges have to do is resign to get completely off the hook. How can there be real justice when judges, who embody justice, conduct themselves in such a despicable manner? Do the harassed women speak up? It takes tremendous courage for them to do so. If they do, either their complaints fall on deaf ears or they face repercussions in the male-dominated system. Women often prefer to maintain their silence.[219]

---

[218]Marina Angel, "Sexual Harassment by Judges," 45 *U Miami L. Rev.* 817 (1991). Web. http://www.law.temple.edu/servlet/com.rnci.products. Data-Modules.RetrievePage?site=TempleLaw&page= N_Faculty_Angel_ publications.

[219]Lorraine Dusky, *Still Unequal: The Shameful Truth about Women and Justice in America* (New York: Crown, 1996). Print.

The U.S. Justice Department and its various divisions, such as the Federal Bureau of Investigation (FBI), the Drug Enforcement Agency (DEA), and the U.S. Marshals, wield tremendous powers in the American courts. The vast majority of people serving in the Justice Department are honest and dedicated citizens, enforcing and upholding the law. But a small fraction of them abuse their power. In his book, David Burnham describes how power is used by a select few. For example, the possession and sale of illegal drugs by police officers, the acceptance of bribes and obstruction of justice by law enforcement agents, improper handling of cases involving illegal dumping of hazardous materials, harassment of lawfully elected minority leaders, and prosecution in less than 0.5 percent of civil rights complaints. There were even plans to suspend the U.S. Constitution under the "Security Portfolio,"[220]

The concept of "white-collar crime" did not exist before World War II. The phrase was first introduced by a sociologist, Edwin Sutherland.[221] Sutherland believed that the criminal activity of the powerful and the well-connected in the business community posed a much greater danger to America than all the murderers, burglars, rapists and muggers. The recent failings of the financial markets and the lip service extended to citizens

---

[220]David Burnham, *Above the Law: Secret Deals, Political Fixes, and Other Misadventures of the U.S. Department of Justice* (New York: Lisa Drew-Scribner, 1996). Print.

[221]"Edwin Sutherland." *Wikipedia, The Free Encyclopedia.* Wikipedia, The Free Encyclopedia, 25 Jun. 2010. Web. 17 July 2010.
http://en.wikipedia.org/wiki/Edwin_Sutherland

during the "Great Recession" bear evidence of that fear expressed by Sutherland more than half a century ago.

Diplomatic Immunity

Another situation in which criminals have more power than the victims is when the criminals are diplomats. They get off the hook for crimes they commit. The United Nations Charter was designed to protect diplomats in foreign countries, especially if the host country was an enemy. But the immunity is abused in order to cover up drug and arms deals. Nations abuse this immunity even to murder exiles living in foreign countries. The murderers, even when caught, have to be released immediately because of their diplomatic immunity. According to data presented by Chuck Ashman and Pamela Trescott in their book *Outrage*, in the U.K. alone, in one year, there were over 250 cases of crimes [including murders] committed by persons claiming diplomatic immunity.[222]

Diplomats also enjoy another kind of privilege: Their bags cannot be searched—even if there is strong suspicion of drug smuggling or importing of contraband goods including smuggling of ancient artifacts. In Article 27 (4) of the UN Charter, it clearly states that a diplomatic bag may only contain diplomatic documents or articles intended for *official* use. Despite this ruling, it seems that Foreign Service has become a den of criminals who abuse their diplomatic immunity for ulterior motives. The extent of the problem can never be known

---

[222]Chuck Ashman and Pamela Trescott, *Outrage: The Abuse of Diplomatic Immunity* (London: Star-W. H. Allen, 1986). Print.

because the Foreign Office or the State Department does not make public all criminal cases involving envoys. According to U.S. Customs officials, art treasures are the second most lucrative illegal material after drugs. The guest nations often ignore or in some cases abet their criminal activity.

SMUGGLING OF ANTIQUES: The plundering and smuggling of antiques from poor nations has been going on for centuries. Approximately 95 percent of ancient art from third-world countries has been hauled in diplomatic bags into wealthy receiving countries such as the U.S. Author Karl E. Meyer has identified prominent members of the high society and famous art collectors, some of whom enjoyed knighthood, or other similar official state titles, who abused their status in plundering ancient temples and other archeological sites.

In the U.S., ancient Mayan artifacts from archeological sites dating back to 800 CE are proudly displayed in museums. The plundering and looting was often supported and funded by "influential friends" of well known museums. An American general used his diplomatic status of Chief Consul to Cyprus in the late 1800s, then under the Ottoman Empire, to plunder and transport over 35,000 pieces of artifacts, which he later sold to the highest bidder, the Metropolitan Museum of New York. He was later appointed the Director of the Metropolitan Museum in 1879.[223]

The most famous example of the abuse of power and privilege of diplomatic status was the plundering and smuggling operation

---

[223]Karl Meyer, *The Plundered Past: The Traffic in Art Treasures* (New York: Penguin, 1977) Print.

conducted in Greece by a British Ambassador in the late 1700s.[224] The plundered pieces were later called the Elgin Marbles. His loot also included a huge assortment of vases and carvings, all transported in diplomatic bags by the Royal Navy. The Elgin marbles became prized possessions of the British Museum.

The business of stolen Indian antiquities is estimated at U.S. $6 billion a year.[225] More than 4000 antiques were stolen in 2006 alone. At least two thousand temples have been plundered and destroyed, while several thousand pieces of sculpture have been smuggled out of the country. In the mid 1900's "pot-hunting" became so fashionable that relief workers from the wealthy nations working for international relief agencies in Third World countries became part of the looting.[226]

What else happens to the treasures of such illicit trade? Do such prized antiques end up in museums where they are proudly displayed, or do they make it to private collections of the privileged in society? Do famous auction houses in the Westernized modern world abet in this trade?[227] Wouldn't

---

[224]"Thomas Bruce, 7th Earl of Elgin." *Wikipedia, The Free Encyclopedia.* Wikipedia, The Free Encyclopedia, 30 May. 2010. Web. 17 July 2010. http://en.wikipedia.org/wiki/Thomas_Bruce,_7th_Earl_of_Elgin

[225]Yatish Yadav, "Stolen, Smuggled, Sold." *Realpolitik.* Web. 24 Oct, 2010. http://www.realpolitik.in/April%2007/Antique.htm

[226]Karl Meyer, *The Plundered Past: The Traffic in Art Treasures* (New York: Penguin, 1977) Print.

[227]Peter Watson, *"Sotheby's – The Inside Story."* New York, Random House, Inc.1997. Print.

global heritage be better served if money were used to preserve and *restore* such ancient treasures?

TRANSPORTATION OF DRUGS, WEAPONS AND CONTRABAND: Is diplomatic cargo also used to carry illegal drugs or to deliver weapons to regions of conflict? There are countries that tacitly support such misuse of the diplomatic privileges. How pervasive is this problem? How can the world hope for a drug-free and peaceful world? The war on drugs and terrorism seems like a charade in the face of such glaring abuse of diplomatic status. Article 36 of the Vienna Convention on Consular Immunity, allows such containers to be searched by the receiving country in the presence of a diplomatic agent.[228] If the permission to search is refused, then it is not allowed entry. So, the truth can never be known. Should the UN conduct spot checks of diplomatic cargo? In a corrupt world, where bribery seems limitless, would such spot checks really solve the problem?

⬜ ⬜ ⬜

Can the citizens of the world expect justice in the face of such blatant abuses by the privileged in society? If law and order are to be preserved and self-proclaimed vigilantes and terrorists are to be discouraged, then it is paramount that the legal system is re-examined. There are compelling reasons to change the way justice is delivered worldwide. A few essential steps in the right direction may help.

---

[228]Vienna Convention on Diplomatic Relations-1961. Web. 25 Sept 2010. http://untreaty.un.org/ilc/texts/instruments/english/conventions/9_1_1961.pdf

In nations that have well-established laws and courts, criminals must not enjoy the same rights as other citizens. More important, courts must endeavor to *seek the truth* and not merely *seek the proof of wrongdoing*. And above all, deliver justice in a timely manner.

Justice and power must be brought together, so that whatever is just may be powerful, and whatever is powerful may be just.

– Blaise Pascal (1623–1662)

French Mathematician, Philosopher and Physicist

Chapter 8
Power and Privilege in Global Politics

Nearly all men can stand adversity, but if you want to test a man's character, give him power.
– Abraham Lincoln: 16th U.S. President (1809 - 1865)

Organizations are formed by like-minded individuals to enhance their power, exercise their will and thereby influence society. Organizations take many forms: religious, political, professional and labor related. Most of them are started by small benevolent groups with good intentions. Some, however, end up being malevolent and destructive. The consequences of their collective strength and misdeeds can be seen all throughout history. Some of them wield tremendous power and sway to change the course of events in the world. A brief review of some of the most influential political organizations of the last century may be a worthwhile exercise, given the precarious geopolitical situation in the world today.

National Politics

SOVIET UNION: The most influential organization of the last century was the Soviet Union, an organization of several soviet republics. Originally, *soviet* was a council of workers. Later the word was adopted for any group formed by citizens to express and exercise their will. Thus, power was supposed to be in the hands of representative councils. Did such a system benefit ordinary people? Did it allow an average citizen to speak out without fear of repercussions?[229]

The Soviet councils, unfortunately, were controlled by leftist (Communist Party) loyalists of the Russian revolution. In effect, the councils became a platform for Communist Party members to implement a hierarchical bureaucratic system that rewarded loyal party activists by giving them leadership roles in running the political institutions, the military, the factories, the educational institutions, etc. Membership in the Party was neither easy nor straightforward. It required indoctrination in the form of special courses, camps, schools, examinations and, most importantly, *nominations by three existing members*. So in the Soviet system, "whom they knew" mattered more than "what they knew" about council matters.

As a result of this clique of loyalists, the Soviet Union became such a closely-knit organization of power-wielding individuals that they could even get away with murder. In order to safeguard their power base, the party leaders needed surveillance to detect signs of disapproval in society. This eventually gave birth to the security agency, the KGB (translates into Committee for State Security), by means of which spying on its own citizenry became the norm.[230] In June, 1918, in the newspaper, *New Life*, the first head of the KGB said: "We

---

[229]"Soviet Union." *Wikipedia, The Free Encyclopedia.* Wikipedia, The Free Encyclopedia, 17 July 2010. Web. 17 July 2010. http://en.wikipedia.org/wiki/Soviet_Union

[230]"KGB." *Wikipedia, The Free Encyclopedia.* Wikipedia, The Free Encyclopedia, 15 July 2010. Web. 17 July 2010. http://en.wikipedia.org/wiki/

represent in ourselves organized terror—this must be said very clearly—such terror is now very necessary in the conditions we are living through in a time of revolution." That started the reign of terror.

Instead of being a participatory representative system, the Soviet Union became a haven for megalomaniacs, foremost among them being Joseph Stalin.[231] With single-party rule and a Soviet system of cronyism, industrialization and collective farming were forced upon the citizens. Those who resisted were incarcerated in gulags to do forced labor. The resistance was strongest among the farmers. It is believed that tens of millions of powerless farmers were executed for resisting. Little wonder the supermarket shelves in the Soviet Union were invariably bare, and citizens often stood in line for bread.

Over time, this yearning for power and control by party members extended beyond its borders. Through annexations, invasions, coercion, occupation and political maneuvering, the Soviet Union by 1956 grew to contain 16 constituent or "union republics:" Armenian, Azerbaijan, Byelorussian, Estonian, Georgian, Kazakh, Kirghiz, Latvian, Lithuanian, Moldavian, Russian, Tajik, Turkmen, Ukrainian, Karelo-Finnish and Uzbek.

Power must evidently blind and intoxicate individuals. The Soviet system ended up doing exactly what it was designed to

[231]"Joseph Stalin." *Wikipedia, The Free Encyclopedia.* Wikipedia, The Free Encyclopedia, 13 July 2010. Web. 17 July 2010.
http://en.wikipedia.org/wiki/Joseph_Stalin

end: oppression of citizens. Meanwhile, party loyalists enjoyed a privileged life of comfort and luxury.

NAZI GERMANY: A notorious political organization that abused its powers in the early twentieth century was the National Socialist German Workers Party of Adolf Hitler (also known as the Nazi Party).[232] After its defeat in World War I (1914-1918), Germany had to sign the Treaty of Versailles in 1919. The treaty blamed former German Emperor Wilhelm II for the war; he was tried, along with other Germans, as a war criminal. Germany not only had to yield control of occupied territories but also was required to pay for war reparations. Also, under the treaty, its armed forces were severely restricted. By the 1930s, German nationalism was on the rise, and the Nazi party became the torchbearer of this nationalistic fervor. The Nazis promoted a Third Way—managed economy that was neither capitalism nor communism.[233]

The 1933 fire in the Reichstag, the German parliament building, was the seminal event that marked the onset of Nazi fascism and abuse of power. The fire was blamed on the Communists, and the arsonist was swiftly tried and convicted. The Reichstag fire was considered suspicious, and rumors were rampant about a possible Nazi conspiracy. According to the archives

---

[232]"Nazi Germany." *Wikipedia, The Free Encyclopedia.* Wikipedia, The Free Encyclopedia, 12 July 2010. Web. 17 July 2010. http://en.wikipedia.org/wiki/Nazi_Germany

[233]"Third Way (Centrism)." *Wikipedia, The Free Encyclopedia.* Wikipedia, The Free Encyclopedia, 11 July 2010. Web. 17 July 2010. http://en.wikipedia. org/wiki/Third_Way_(centrism)

held in Moscow, and made available to researchers only since 1990, the fire was almost certainly started by the Nazis themselves, and blamed on Communists to win popular support. Interestingly, in 1981, the West German courts posthumously acquitted the formerly accused arsonist. Justice was delayed by almost half century.

At the time, the Nazi Party[234] used the fire as an excuse to terrorize and massacre suspected Communist insurgents. Hitler called the fire a "sign from heaven," and warned that it was a signal of a Communist plot. The Nazis, who believed in the failure of democracy, failure of capitalism, and the "racial purity of the German people," unleashed an era of horrors throughout the region that was to last 12 long years.[235]

Here is how it was all orchestrated. In 1933, they passed the Reichstag Fire Decree, the law rescinding *habeas corpus* and other civil liberties. Most ordinary Germans condoned such transgressions by officials and violation of their rights. Their smugness came from an improving economy and a comfortable standard of living. Eventually, all political opposition was crushed with widespread eavesdropping by Nazi spies. Thousands of German citizens were imprisoned and many were tortured and killed. Special courts were appointed to try and sentence

---

[234]"Adolf Hitler." *Wikipedia, The Free Encyclopedia*. Wikipedia, The Free Encyclopedia, 17 July 2010. Web. 17 July 2010.
http://en.wikipedia.org/wiki/Adolf_Hitler

[235]"Nazi Germany." *Wikipedia, The Free Encyclopedia*. Wikipedia, The Free Encyclopedia, 17 July 2010. Web. 17 July 2010.
http://en.wikipedia.org/wiki/Nazi_Germany

dissenters. Between 1933 and 1945, millions of German citizens were sentenced to death by the oppressive regime.

The year 1933 also marked the passage of another law: The Enabling Act, which empowered Hitler and made him a dictator. Hitler and his fascist followers soon created the Secret Police—the Gestapo, under the administration of the elite protection squadron, the Schutz Staffel, i.e. the SS.[236] A year later, in 1934, another act, the Gesetz über den Neuaufbau des Reichs (Act to Rebuild the Reich), was passed by the Nazis, which further consolidated Hitler's power. The act changed the highly decentralized federal Germany into a centralized state with only one political party. It empowered the Nazis to disband state parliaments, transferring sovereign rights of the various states to the central government, and the state administrations came under the control of the Reich administration. Additional laws ended autonomies of cities and towns, and the mayors of towns were appointed by the (Nazi) Interior Minister.

At first the SS targeted the Jews because the Nazis believed the humiliating defeat in WWI was caused by the Jews. The rights of Jews were increasingly restricted. Jews were not allowed to work in the civil service, Jewish physicians were not allowed to practice medicine, Jews were barred from owning farms, Jewish lawyers were disbarred, and Jews were not allowed to attend schools and universities. Eventually, they were even stripped of their citizenship. The pro-Nazi newspaper,

---

[236]"Schutzstaffel." *Wikipedia, The Free Encyclopedia.* Wikipedia, The Free Encyclopedia, 12 July 2010. Web. 17 July 2010.
http://en.wikipedia.org/wiki/Schutzstaffel

Deutsche Allgemeine Zeitung in April 27, 1933, wrote: "A self-respecting nation cannot, on a scale accepted up to now, leave its higher activities in the hands of people of racially foreign origin. . . . Allowing the presence of too high a percentage of people of foreign origin in relation to their percentage in the general population could be interpreted as an acceptance of the superiority of other races, something decidedly to be rejected."

In order to carry out its agenda, the SS created a special procedure to incarcerate people without judicial proceedings, calling it protective custody. Strangely enough, the prisoners signed their own imprisonment orders—obviously out of fear of personal harm. Thus, power was abused in order to round up, imprison, and execute millions of innocent people. The "undesirable" people of Nazi genocidal policies included Jews (an estimated 6 million), the Poles, the Romany (gypsies), Slavs, Serbs, Soviets, homosexuals, Communists and other political prisoners, Jehovah's Witnesses, Freemasons, and disabled people believed by the Nazis to have a worthless life. Even the elderly, women, and children were not exempt.

All the "undesirable" people were sent to concentration camps where they were starved and denied basic amenities. Quite a few died of disease and starvation. The rest were systematically killed. The methods used to rid Europe of these "undesirable" people were ghastly. One favored method of killing was the gas chamber. The prisoners were stripped naked and sent to gas chambers where they were killed by carbon monoxide poisoning. Thousands of disabled and ill inmates were forced into locked stables, which were doused with kerosene and set ablaze, burning alive all those inside. Other prisoners were led in groups to ravines in nearby forests and shot in the neck.

What point does it serve to describe these atrocities, especially since they have been talked about many, many times before? Refreshing this memory, every now and then, is necessary, lest responsible pro-democracy citizens, especially the youth, in the free world become too complacent and allow history to repeat itself.

The SS extended its tentacles beyond Germany's borders into what are now 35 separate European countries. It is generally agreed that by the end of World War II (WWII), between 11 and 17 million people, and perhaps as high as 21 million people, may have been systematically killed by the Nazis in a span of 12 years ending in 1945.[237] Unlike any previous ethnic purges throughout history, the victims of the Nazis were not able to escape death by converting to another religion or assimilating into the prevalent culture.

In its war against the Soviets in the eastern theater during WWII, the Nazis were directly or indirectly responsible for 20 million deaths of Soviet civilians and seven million Red Army soldiers. It also claimed the lives of 5.5 million German soldiers; their bodies strewn all over the European landscape generated little or no pity. The Nazis, who were so blinded by their power, had envisioned displacing 51 million Slavic people in the event of their victory in the War.

---

[237]"World War II." *Wikipedia, The Free Encyclopedia.* Wikipedia, The Free Encyclopedia, 14 July 2010. Web. 17 July 2010.
http://en.wikipedia.org/wiki/World_War_II

World War II was the bloodiest war in history, during which 50 to 72 million people lost their lives; over four million were Americans. The victors of WWII declared the Nazi Party a criminal organization which ultimately brought an end to the regime.

Despite such a ghastly record in history, the Nazis have a following in the United Sates of America. The American Nazi Party (ANP), an organization founded by George Lincoln Rockwell in 1960, aimed to revive Nazi white supremacist fervor and deny the World War II Holocaust.[238] There is a resurgence of such organizations in the UK, Italy, Germany, Japan and Sweden.

The World Union of National Socialists (WUNS) that espouses the Third Position, just like the Nazis, already has members in the following countries (in alphabetical order): Argentina, Australia, Austria, Belgium, Britain, Chile, France, Ireland, Japan, South Africa and the U.S.[239] In addition, it allegedly has affiliation with a number of minor movements all over the world. Most of them are nationalist organizations, favoring the Third Position that is opposed to both communism and capitalism. However, could fascist elements infiltrate such organizations? Americans and freedom-loving people all over the world ought to be more vigilant about organizations based on

[238]"American Nazi Party." *Wikipedia, The Free Encyclopedia.* Wikipedia, The Free Encyclopedia, 16 July 2010. Web. 17 July 2010.
http://en.wikipedia.org/wiki/American_Nazi_Party

[239]"World Union of National Socialists." *Wikipedia, The Free Encyclopedia.* Wikipedia, The Free Encyclopedia, 9 Apr. 2010. Web. 17 July 2010.
http://en.wikipedia.org/wiki/World_Union_of_National_Socialists

fascist, albeit nationalist, principles of the Nazis. Many of them appear to be Internet-based. The stealth penetration into our democracy by fascist organizations through cyberspace may escape the attention of the unaware.

UNITED STATES OF AMERICA: In the U.S., the founding fathers carefully drafted the U.S. Constitution to vest all legislative power in Congress, which consists of the Senate and the House of Representatives. Senators and Representatives are chosen by direct elections in every state of the Union.[240] Sensing the potential abuse of power by the U.S. Presidency, Congress has restricted the powers of the President with laws such as the Congressional Budget and Impoundment Control Act of 1974 and the War Powers Resolution.[241, 242] Nevertheless, the U.S. President remains considerably powerful, and controlled by the powerful. How can that be in the greatest democracy in the world? That is because the U.S. presidential election is not controlled by its citizens. Here is how.

The U.S. is a Union of component states. Therefore, to maintain the coalition of states, the power to elect the U.S. President and Vice President is vested in the individual states and *not the average citizen*. Therefore, under the Constitution, the

---

[240]"The United States Congress." *Wikipedia, The Free Encyclopedia.* Wikipedia, The Free Encyclopedia. 22 Sept. 2010. Web. 22 Sept 2010.

[241]"Congressional Budget and Impoundment Control Act of 1974." *Wikipedia, the Free Encyclopedia.* Wikipedia, the Free Encyclopedia. 17 Sept. 2010. Web. 22 Sept 2010.

[242]"War Powers Resolution" *Wikipedia, the Free Encyclopedia.* Wikipedia, the Free Encyclopedia. 29 July 2010. Web. 22 Sept 2010.

highest elected official that average American citizens can elect, by direct popular vote, are governors of their states—and not the nation's president. Only the electors from individual states, belonging to the State Electoral Colleges, elect the U.S. President and Vice-President.[243] In other words, the nationwide popular vote is not the basis for electing a President or Vice President.

The U.S. Constitution delegates to each state full authority for *nominating* and choosing its electors. Accordingly, most states allow the political parties, specifically, Democrat and Republican, to nominate electors during the months prior to Election Day. Thus, the power to elect a president is controlled by power-wielding insiders of the two dominant political parties—not the average citizens. This process virtually eliminates the possibility of independent candidates or even third-party candidates from winning the U.S. presidency.

Are the candidacies of other parties or Independents a charade? Not quite. Neither the U.S. Constitution, nor any state law compels the state electors to vote for any particular candidate based on popular vote of the State or for the candidate of their nominating party. So, *in theory*, the electors could vote for an independent or third-party candidate. But would they dare vote for a candidate who does not belong to the two powerful parties that control the nomination process? Is it remotely possible that electors could be bought to vote a certain way? Is there

---

[243]"Electoral College (United States)." *Wikipedia, the Free Encyclopedia.* Wikipedia, the Free Encyclopedia, 16 July 2010. Web. 17 July 2010. http://en.wikipedia.org/wiki/Electoral_College_(United_States)

room for *quid pro quo*? Could the system get corrupted, or become vulnerable to outside manipulation in the future?

Lately, the differences between the two political parties seem to be blurring. The political debates seem focused on a few social issues such as abortion and gay marriage. Therefore, the system is beginning to resemble a one-party system heavily controlled by campaign contributions. Winning not only the nomination but also the election is clearly related to the amount of money raised by candidates. Thus, the elected officials of the U.S. Congress, as well as the U.S. president, are beholden to big campaign contributors. In other words, elected officials, including the president, are being bought with money.

Wouldn't it be better to reform the practice of campaign contributions in the U.S? Attempts to do so have met with little success. Hundreds of millions of dollars are being paid, and will continue to be paid, for the campaigns of candidates every election year. Such contributions are in defiance of the Federal Election Campaign Act (FECA) of 1971 and its 1974 amendment limiting election contributions.[244, 245] The Act led to the creation of the Federal Election Commission (FEC). According to the 2008 FEC laws, no candidate or political committee could knowingly accept any contribution or make any expenditure in violation of the provisions of [the law]. For example, according to Article 441b of the FEC law, it was unlawful for

---

[244] *FEC.* Federal Election Commission, n.d.. Web. 17 July 2010. http://www.fec.gov/

[245] Federal Election Campaign Act, *Wikipedia, the Free Encyclopedia.* Wikipedia, the Free Encyclopedia, 27 Oct. 2010. Web. 28 Oct 2010

any national bank, or any corporation, or any labor organization to make any political contribution. In addition, according to Article 441c of the law, it was unlawful for any individual who entered into any contract with the U.S. government or its agencies to directly or indirectly make any contribution of money or other things of value. Furthermore, according to Article 441e, it was unlawful for a foreign national, directly or indirectly, to make a contribution or donation of money, or any other item of value. And last, but not least, according to Article 441g, no person could make contributions of currency of the U.S. or currency of any foreign country to or for the benefit of any candidate, which, in the aggregate, exceeds $100, with respect to any campaign of such candidate for nomination for election or for election to Federal office.[246]

To an average citizen, the law seems rather straightforward. But there are experts who have invented ways to get around the law and find loopholes and make it their business to raise millions of dollars of campaign money and defeat the purpose of the law.

Until recently, corporations and organizations could contribute only "soft money" to a political party of their choice [as opposed to "hard money" paid directly to the candidates]. How much "soft money" is used to buy American presidents?

---

[246]Federal Election Campaign Laws April 2008.
http://www.fec.gov/law/feca/feca.pdf

The following table reveals the campaign contributions reported to the Federal Election Commission (FEC) by the two leading parties in 2004 (the numbers are rounded off).

Category	Donations to Republican (U.S. $)	Donations to Democrat (U.S. $)
Agricultural sector	3.9 million	375 thousand
Defense contractors	655 thousand	173 thousand
Utility	3.9 million	373 thousand
Labor unions	46 thousand	106 thousand
Construction industry	7.3 million	1.2 million
Communications and Electronics	4.4 million	5 million
Financial sector, Insurance and Real Estate	28 million	7.9 million
Healthcare	8.5 million	3.4 million
Trial lawyers and Lobbyists (PACS)	10.6 million	12.8 million
Airlines and other transportation	4 million	381 thousand
Miscellaneous (Religious groups)	38.4 million	14.8 million

(Figures courtesy of http://www.opensecrets.org/ – Center for Responsive Politics).[247]

One way corporations wield power in the U.S. democracy is by sponsoring candidates to speak to all their employees (and

---

[247]*Open Secrets Blog.* Center for Responsive Politics, n.d. Web. 17 July 2010. http://www.opensecrets.org/

the public), which is legal as long as the corporations do not openly endorse a candidate. Moreover, the candidate may not collect contributions at such meetings, but can leave campaign paraphernalia, including stamped envelopes for contributors to use. What a circuitous and wasteful way of dodging the law. Do such corporations give an equal opportunity to all the candidates to raise campaign funds? Or, do they simply invite those who have tacitly agreed to look out for the interests of the company if elected?

Another creative way of getting around the laws of campaign contributions is through the creation by big corporations of a special category of a restricted class of employees who are either shareholders or have administrative roles. Candidates are invited to speak to this restricted class. At such meetings, the candidates seek votes, ask for contributions, and recruit volunteers to operate telephone banks to urge other citizens to vote for or against a candidate. All of this seems participatory on the surface, but the restricted class of employees is obviously beholden to the corporations.

A loophole exists in the law that "does not prohibit or make unlawful the establishment or administration of, or the solicitation of contributions to, any *separate segregated fund* (SS fund) by any corporation, labor organization . . . for the purpose of influencing the nomination for election, or election, of any person to Federal office." In other words, corporations and organizations could create a separate account for money to be used for campaign contributions. The account could be funded by the restricted class of employees up to $5,000 each per year. By so doing, between elections each restricted employee could contribute $20,000 to the account. Could some of the funds be collected by mandatory payroll deductions?

How is the money from SS funds dispersed? The money is siphoned through a private entity called a political action committee (PAC), which then openly extends financial support to candidates.[248] In other words, when a special interest group or an organization wants to make political contributions, it creates a PAC in order to legally make campaign contributions. It is believed that PACs account for less than 30 percent of total contributions in U.S. Congressional races, and considerably less in presidential races. Nevertheless, the amount of money contributed by PACs is staggering. Here are the figures on the size of campaign contributions by PACs: between 2002 and 2004, $915.7 million; between 2004 and 2006, $1.1 billion; and in the last election of 2008, $1.2 billion. At the end of the 2008 election, PACs had $308.6 million still left over.

---

[248]"Political Action Committee." *Wikipedia, The Free Encyclopedia.* Wikipedia, The Free Encyclopedia, 9 Jun. 2010. Web. 17 July 2010. http://en.wikipedia.org/wiki/Political_action_committee

The table below lists the top 20 organizations that paid PAC money in the 2008 elections made public by the FEC. The list shows the sway in the two political parties. (Details can be viewed on the website of Center for Responsive Politics: www.opensecrets.org.)

PAC Name	Total	Democrat	Republican
National Assn of Realtors	$4,013,900	58 percent	42 percent
Intl Brotherhood of Electrical Workers	$3,344,600	98 percent	2 percent
AT&T Inc.	$3,108,200	47 percent	52 percent
National Auto Dealers Assn	$2,864,000	34 percent	66 percent
National Beer Wholesalers Assn.	$2,860,000	53 percent	47 percent
American Bankers Assn	$2,834,600	42 percent	58 percent
International Assn of Fire Fighters	$2,703,900	77 percent	23 percent
American Assn for Justice	$2,700,500	95 percent	4 percent
Operating Engineers Union	$2,692,600	87 percent	13 percent
Laborers Union	$2,540,300	92 percent	8 percent
Honeywell International	$2,512,100	52 percent	48 percent
National Assn of Home Builders	$2,482,000	46 percent	54 percent
Air Line Pilots Assn	$2,387,000	85 percent	15 percent
Machinists/Aerospace Workers Union	$2,326,800	97 percent	3 percent
Credit Union National Assn	$2,313,500	53 percent	47 percent
Plumbers/Pipefitters Union	$2,304,600	95 percent	5 percent
Service Employees International Union	$2,287,200	94 percent	6 percent
American Federation of Teachers	$2,279,700	99 percent	1 percent
Teamsters Union	$2,257,000	97 percent	3 percent
Nat. Air Traffic Contr. Assn.	$2,226,400	80 percent	20 percent

How else do big businesses influence legislation? They do so by either directly hiring former elected officials and their staff members or by hiring lobbying firms to do their job. Big corporations, lobbying firms, and special interest groups are also quick to hire defeated candidates and their staff members after every election. They also hire former employees of other Federal agencies to influence how the U.S. government conducts its business.[249] Such lobbying firms have created a revolving door of sorts that "shuffles former federal employees (and elected officials) into jobs as lobbyists, consultants and strategists just as the door pulls former hired guns into government careers." Thus, elected officials and their inside staff members "spin in and out of the private and public sectors, so too does privilege, power, access and, of course, money."[250]

Such revolving doors also exist between the Pentagon and defense contractors, whereby retired senior officers work as consultants for the Pentagon (as members of the Defense Policy Board), and are employed by Defense contractors, while still collecting a pension.[251]

---

[249]Melissa Rossi, *What Every American Should Know About Who's Really Running the World: The People, Corporations, and Organizations That Control Our Future* (New York: Plume-Penguin, 2005). Print.

[250]Revolving door, Opensecrets.org Center for Responsive Politics blog. Web. 20 July 2010. http://www.opensecrets.org/revolving/

[251]*Profiting from Access* – Cover Story, USA Today, December 15, 2009

Could the well-connected power-wielding recruits manipulate the decisions made by the Pentagon, the Defense Policy Board, or the U.S. Congress? The goals of the lobbying firms are determined by the clients they serve and include procuring government contracts and influencing the outcome of votes in the Senate and the House that may affect their clients. Every responsible citizen of the world ought to see the documentary, "Casino Jack and the United States of Money" (producer and director Alex Gibney, Magnolia Pictures. 2009). It sheds light on unholy alliances between big business and elected officials. A website designed to help citizens check out the corruption of elected officials is also well worth a visit:

   http://www. participantmedia.com/social_action/
   casino_jack/campaign.php.

Also, a citizens' database on the website,

   http://www.opensecrets.org/revolving/index.php,

tracks anyone whose résumé includes positions of influence in both the private and public sectors. Should "We, the People," be examining the data before every vote? Yes, if democracy is to be preserved.

So who really wields power in the U.S. democracy: the average citizen, labor organizations, or the big corporations? One could argue that corporations actually represent average citizens who are shareholders. But do they really represent shareholder interests? It may be worthwhile to read Chapter 5 again. Besides, follow the billions of bailout dollars given to the banking industry in 2008, as well as other major failing corporations and the answer will become apparent. There is a mere trickle of money making its way from "Wall Street to Main Street."[252]

Healthy, participatory democracy in the U.S. suffered a huge blow in January 2010. The U.S. Supreme Court made it legal for corporations to make *direct* campaign contributions.[253] This ruling must feel like adding insult to injury to average Americans who believed that the elections were not fair and open to begin with. The Democratic President called the Supreme Court ruling, "a major victory for big oil, Wall Street banks, health insurance companies and the other powerful interests that marshal their power every day in Washington to drown out the voices of everyday Americans."[254] Time alone will tell how the ruling will play out in future elections.

Could foreign powers manipulate U.S. elections? The possibility is very real, particularly after the January 2010 Supreme Court Ruling on corporate campaign donations. The FECA bans contributions by foreigners including foreign governments, foreign political parties, foreign corporations, foreign associations, foreign partnerships, individuals with foreign citizenship,

---

[252]Matthew Ericson, Elaine He, and Amy Schoenfeld. "Tracking the $700 Billion Bailout." *NYTimes.* The New York Times, n.d. Web. 17 July 2010. http://projects.nytimes.com/creditcrisis/recipients/table

[253]Adam Liptak, "Justices, 5-4, Reject Corporate Spending Limit." *NY Times.* New York Times, 21 Jan. 2010. Web. 23 July 2010. http://www.nytimes.com/2010/01/22/us/politics/22scotus.html

[254]James Vicini, "Landmark Supreme Court ruling allows corporate political cash." *Reuters.* 21 Jan 2010. Web. 22 Sept 2010. http://www.reuters.com/article/idUSTRE60K3SK20100121

and immigrants who do not have a permanent resident status.[255] Despite the ban, there are currently over 120 foreign PACs. In the 2008 elections, foreign PACs contributed over US$14 million ($7,036,905 to Democrats, and $7,457,791 to Republicans).

Further details are available on the website:

http://www.opensecrets.org/pacs/foreign.php

After the September 11, 2001 (9/11), terrorist attacks, democracy in the country seems further threatened. There are some people who consider the 9/11 attacks as a conspiracy—similar to the Nazi conspiracy of the Reichstag fire.[256] A few parallels between the Nazi German modus operandi and the recent events in the U.S. seem noteworthy. The 9/11 attacks were viewed by some as the seminal event, much like the fateful German fire. Critics who believe so think the U.S. government knew about the impending attacks, but chose not to act, whereas others believe a private network of powerful high-level officials within the U.S. Government carried out the attacks. The motives allegedly were to use the attacks as a pretext to justify war, to increase military spending, and to restrict domestic civil liberties. Does this all sound similar to the events that took place in Nazi Germany? The truth will never be known, but the parallels are indeed disturbing.

---

[255]Foreign Nationals, July 2003. Federal Election Commission. Web 20 July 2010. http://www.fec.gov/pages/brochures/foreign.shtml

[256]"9/11 Conspiracy Theories." *Wikipedia, The Free Encyclopedia.* Wikipedia, The Free Encyclopedia, 3 July 2010. Web. 17 July 2010. http://en.wikipedia.org/wiki/9/11_conspiracy_theories

Post 9/11, the U.S. domestic policy was aimed at restricting civil liberties, just as in the former Soviet Union and Nazi Germany. The passage of the law called Uniting and Strengthening America by Providing Appropriate Tools Required to Intercept and Obstruct Terrorism Act of 2001 was successfully carried out even though it violated the U.S. Constitution.[257] The Act has a remarkable acronym: USA PATRIOT Act. It suggests nationalist and patriotic sentiments. So the opponents of the Act could be conveniently labeled unpatriotic. Even though the Federal courts have ruled a number of provisions of the Act as unconstitutional, and although the Act was to be temporary, ending on December 31, 2005, it remains in effect even today. The Act became permanent, with only minor modifications, duly approved by the US Congress and signed by former President George W. Bush. The original language of the Act remains untouched in most sections despite protests by elected officials in Congress.

One of the biggest controversies of the USA PATRIOT Act is that it allows surveillance of U.S. citizens by the FBI without a court order. All the FBI has to do is merely generate a National Security Letter (NSL) and demand any information, on anybody, from anybody. In other words, it can tap telephone, e-mail, library and financial records of any U.S. citizen. The American Civil Liberties Union (ACLU) has challenged the constitutionality of NSLs in court. The American Library Association condemned the USA PATRIOT Act, and urged members to

---

[257]"USA PATRIOT Act." *Wikipedia, The Free Encyclopedia*. Wikipedia, The Free Encyclopedia, 16 July 2010. Web. 17 July 2010.
http://en.wikipedia.org/wiki/USA_PATRIOT_Act

defend free speech and protect their patrons' privacy. To that end, some librarians have started shredding records to avoid having to comply with such orders. Supporters of the Act argue that such overarching laws are needed to deal with terrorism and that racial profiling is a necessary evil. Average citizens all over the world can only hope that terrorism is not manufactured to suit the hidden agenda or greed of a select group of people.

Another controversial aspect of the USA PATRIOT Act is the indefinite detention, without a trial, of any alien—including legal immigrants—the Attorney General believes may conduct a terrorist act. Could this act be abused, if not today, sometime in the future? The University of California has passed a resolution condemning such indefinite detentions without a trial. In addition, the ACLU has accused that the Act gives the Attorney General "unprecedented new power to determine the fate of immigrants . . . Worse yet, if the foreigners do not have a country that will accept them, they can be detained indefinitely without trial."[258]

What is even more alarming is that the USA PATRIOT Act also affects citizens of the sovereign nation north of the U.S. border.[259] The citizens of the Canadian province, British

---

[258] *ACLU Releases Comprehensive Report On Patriot Act Abuse*-March 11 2009. Web. July 20 2010. http://www.aclu.org/national-security/aclu-releases-comprehensive-report-patriot-act-abuses

[259] Michelle Kisluk and Wendy Gross, "Canada's Privacy Laws vs. The USA PATRIOT ACT." *FindLaw*. Findlaw, 2010. Web. 17 July 2010. http://library.findlaw.com/2005/May/10/245866.html

Columbia, are concerned that the Act will allow the United States government to access Canadians' private information from companies that have outsourced to American companies. Therefore, to further safeguard the privacy of its citizens, British Columbia made amendments to its existing Freedom of Information and Protection of Privacy Act (FOIPPA), which was enacted as law on October 21, 2004. The maximum penalty for violating the provisions of the law has a fine of $500,000. However, the amendments only protect public sector data, and do not cover private sector data in Canada. Similar legal action was also taken by concerned Canadians in Nova Scotia to protect them against the USA PATRIOT Act. On November 15, 2007, they also passed legislation to protect Nova Scotians' personal information from being violated by the USA PATRIOT ACT. The new law was the Personal Information International Disclosure Protection Act.[260] The law specifies the responsibilities of public sector officials in protecting citizens' personal information, and the consequences if these responsibilities are not fulfilled.

Enemies of democracy and terrorist elements could well be lurking in America's neighborhoods, awaiting an opportune time to strike. The threat seems very real. The New York's Time Square bomber is a case in point.[261] Clearly, there is a need to

---

[260]"Nova Scotia USA Patriot Act Response is Back on!" *Canadian Privacy Law Blog*. 11 July 2006. Web. 17 July 2010.
http://www.privacylawyer.ca/blog/2006/07/nova-scotia-usa-patriot-act-response.html

[261]"U.S. Arrests Three in Times Square Bomb Probe." Reuters. Thompson Reuters, 13 May 2010. Web. 17 July 2010.
http://www.reuters.com/article/idUSN1327123720100514

protect citizens from such terrorists residing in the country. But could powerful, foreign forces infiltrate the system to destroy American democracy from within? Could terrorists be custom-tailored by such anti-American agenda? Has the USA PATRIOT Act created loopholes for the potential abuse of power without checks and balances?

Fortunately, well-meaning and enlightened people are a majority, and the best years of democracy have yet to come. The poem below is worth a thousand words.

America
Centre of equal daughters, equal sons,
All, alike endear'd, grown, ungrown, young and old,
Strong, ample, fair, enduring, capable, rich,
Perennial with the Earth, with Freedom, Law and Love,
A grand, sane, towering, seated Mother,
Chair'd in the adamant of Time
– Walt Whitman (1919-1892)[262]

CHINA: Today, in the People's Republic of China (PROC), i.e., mainland (Communist) China, individual freedom is severely curtailed. The power to control the masses in China rests with the People's Liberation Army (PLA).[263] How can an organization like the PLA become so powerful? It all started with the fall of the last Imperial dynasty in 1911. The country was overrun by warlords at the time and, in 1927, civil war broke out with two dominant factions: one supported by the West and the

---

[262]Walt Whitman – *Leaves of Grass*. Random House, Inc. New York. 2001.

[263]http://en.wikipedia.org/wiki/Peoplepercent27s_Republic_of_China

other by the Communist Soviet Union. The protracted civil war is called War of Liberation in the PROC. During this period, over a span of 47 years, the Chinese people witnessed over 175 minor and major wars, armed insurgencies, armed conflicts and military campaigns. Eventually, Soviet aid succeeded in establishing Chinese communism—and its power base, the PLA. The nation, under the tutelage of the PLA, turned into one of oppression and brutality. Over the course of decades, the power-wielding PLA under the leadership of Mao Zedong[264] carried out rural and urban purges of its own citizens. It is estimated that the cost in human lives of establishing PLA's power base in communist China is 35–80 million deaths.[265] The War of Liberation also displaced nearly 2 million non-communist, nationalist Chinese, led by Chiang Kai-shek, to the island of Taiwan.[266] What or who was the PLA *liberating the people* from? Things have not changed much over time. The oppressive Communist regime still curtails individual freedoms. For example, on April 15, 1989, approximately 1 million citizens gathered to mourn the death of pro-democracy leader Hu Yao-bang in Beijing's Tiananmen Square. The protestors included students and intellectuals, as well as some Communist Party

---

[264]"Mao Zedong." *Wikipedia, The Free Encyclopedia.* Wikipedia, The Free Encyclopedia, 17 July 2010. Web. 17 July 2010.
http://en.wikipedia.org/wiki/Mao_Zedong

[265]Robert Walker – Human Cost of Communism in China – 1971 - Report to the U.S. Senate Committee; Le Vivre Noir du Communisme; Jung Chang – Mao: the Unknown Story - 2005

[266]"Republic of China." *Wikipedia, The Free Encyclopedia.* Wikipedia, The Free Encyclopedia, 16 July 2010. Web. 17 July 2010.
http://en.wikipedia.org/wiki/Republic_of_China

leaders. On June 4, the protestors were mowed down by the PLA, which killed hundreds, if not thousands. The actual death toll of the uprising remains a guarded secret to this day. The PLA wields so much power that on the twentieth anniversary of the Tiananmen Square uprising even Internet-based Twitter and Hotmail were blocked.[267]

The 2010 Nobel Peace Prize was awarded to a Chinese democracy advocate, Liu Xiaobo, who has been responsible for a peaceful and non-violent struggle for human rights in China. But the oppressive Communist regime treated the award with contempt rather than pride. The regime even threatened to cut off diplomatic relations with Norway.[268]

INDIA: Democracy in India is threatened by the inner workings of the various political parties. According to a senior leader of the one such party, "Democracy in political parties is non-existent in India. You cannot enter [politics] unless you are well connected." She contends that seats for the Parliamentary elections are "up for bidding as opposed to a meritocratic appointment to run [for office in an election]." In retaliation for revealing the truth, she was stripped of her administrative role in

---

[267]"Tiananmen Square Protests of 1989." *Wikipedia, The Free Encyclopedia.* Wikipedia, The Free Encyclopedia, 9 July 2010. Web. 17 July 2010. http://en.wikipedia.org/wiki/Tiananmen_Square_protests_of_1989

[268]Sharon K. Hom, "China snubs courageous Nobel Peace prize." CNN. 8 Oct. 2010. Web. 14 Oct 2010. http://articles.cnn.com/2010-10-08/opinion/ hom.nobel.china_1_liu-xiaobo-china-snubs-chinese-government? _s=PM:OPINION

the party.[269] Such bartering for parliamentary seats goes on in all political parties as well. So it seems that even in India—a multi-party, Parliamentary secular democracy—the power to become a candidate, let alone win the election, is ultimately determined by the well-connected wealthy and powerful. And they keep the elected officials as well as the state employees like dogs on short leashes. What is the advantage of having a one-person-one-vote democracy? India is turning into a democracy where the government does not heed the consent of its governed. It has begun to represent the interests of the wealthy and the powerful and special interest groups. Is such a system vulnerable to outside manipulation?

Democracy in India is also threatened by the ugly politics of religion. Even though India has had a *secular* democratic constitution since its independence in 1947, the Muslims have been given the right to apply Muslim Personal (*Sharia*) Law. One major point of contention among the majority in India is the power wielded by the male-dominated Muslim political parties and religious organizations to safeguard the applicability of the *Sharia* law in a secular democratic India. The All India Muslim Personal Law Board (AIMPLB) is one such organization formed in 1973.[270] The power of AIMPLB was brought forth after the 1978 Shah Bano divorce case. The 69-year-old Muslim woman, Shah Bano, demanded alimony

---

[269]"Margaret Alva." *Wikipedia, The Free Encyclopedia*. Wikipedia, The Free Encyclopedia, 13 Jun. 2010. Web. 18 July 2010.
http://en.wikipedia.org/wiki/Margaret_Alva

[270]*AIMPLB*. All India Muslim Personal Law Board, 7-8 Apr. 1973. Web. 17 July 2010. http://www.aimplboard.org/

granted to Indian women in accordance with Indian secular law. The case reached the Indian Supreme Court which granted the alimony to the divorcée. The orthodox [male] Muslims in India felt threatened by the ruling and protested widely. The goal of AIMPLB as a private body is to protect *Sharia* laws, dictated by powerful male religious leaders, to be applied to all Muslims—even those who may prefer to live by the secular laws of the country. How safe is Indian democracy in the midst of such male-dominated, power-wielding organizations? Why do the Indian Muslims fail to realize that their ancestors may have been forcibly converted to Islam? Could enemy nations be funding such organizations to manipulate Indian democracy? To counterbalance the sway of Muslim organizations, Hindus too have formed their own religious organizations. The situation is no different than that in Northern Ireland where the Catholics and Protestants have fruitlessly tried to dominate the politics of the country. Hopefully, the less fanatic religious organizations, such as the All India Muslim Women's Personal Law Board, will see the wisdom of a secular parliamentary democracy while preserving Islamic life styles based on the Holy Qur'an. One can only hope that with Muslims embracing secular laws of India there will be "sudden death" of reactionary and radical Hindu organizations. Then perhaps there can be real peace and harmony.

In Indian democracy, the established political parties and their leaders have little interest in governance. In early 2010, India's upper house, the Rajya Sabha, wisely approved a bill that would reserve one-third of Parliamentary seats for women.[271]

---

[271]Jason Burke. "Indian Parliament Approves Plan for Women's Quota." *Guardian.* Guardian, 9 Mar. 2010. Web. 17 July 2010.
http://www.guardian.co.uk/world/2010/mar/09/india-parliament-approves-female-quota

According to a female Member of Parliament, Mallika Sarabhai, the entrenched male politicians complained that the women members would merely be the "rubber stamp" of their husbands. Do the entrenched, self-serving, male members of the Parliament fail to see that they are already rubber stamps of the wealthy and powerful?

To fight terrorism, in 2002, the Indian government enacted the Prevention of Terrorism Act (POTA).[272] But the law is being misused by political leaders to further their personal goals. It is used to silence criticism of the government, clamp down on political opposition, for ethnic cleansing, to imprison indigenous people fighting for their land, to conduct secret trials not open to the public and to torture prisoners.[273] There are reports of encounters with special police, systematic disappearances, custodial deaths, rape and gang rape of voiceless Indian citizens. Is Indian democracy safe under POTA?

TALIBAN, AL-QAEDA AND THEIR ALLIES: Taliban means "student" in Pashto, a language spoken by the Pashtuns in Afghanistan. When first organized by Mullah Omar in 1994, Taliban was an organization of average Pashtuns and students of Islam dedicated to oust corrupt, cruel and malicious warlords in various parts of southern Afghanistan. Within several months, the small group of Taliban gained control over 34 southern provinces, unseating local warlords and imposing a strict Islamic life style on citizens.

---

[272]"Prevention of Terrorist Activities Act." *Wikipedia, The Free Encyclopedia*. Wikipedia, The Free Encyclopedia, 11 July 2010. Web. 17 July 2010. http://en.wikipedia.org/wiki/Prevention_of_Terrorist_Activities_Act

[273]Arundhati Roy; *An ordinary person's guide to Empire* – Penguin books India 2005. Print.

The situation was different in northern Afghanistan. After the defeat of Communists and Soviets in 1989 at the hands of *mujahideens* (holy warriors), and the forces of the Northern Alliance (also called the United Front), there was establishment of the Islamic State of Afghanistan (ISA) with its capital based in Kabul. The Northern Alliance and the Kabul government were duly recognized by the UN and most foreign countries. The success of ousting the Communists from Afghanistan was accomplished with the help of the brave *mujahideens* who allegedly received covert support from the CIA and Pakistan's Inter-Services Intelligence (ISI).

In 1996, the Taliban, emboldened by their victories in southern Afghanistan successfully invaded Kabul and started their oppressive rule. The Taliban imposed its own style of Islam, denying human rights, massacring Shi'ites and Hazar Muslims, subjugating women, operating terrorist training camps, exporting terror to neighboring countries. It banned all pork products, radios, tapes and recorders, televisions, satellite dishes, photography, cinema, musical instruments, statues, pictures and paintings of living things, including Christmas cards, among other things. Girls were denied an education after age 8, and women could not work outside their homes. It imposed a strict dress code for men and women: the men had to grow long beards but had to wear short hair on their heads; women were expected to wear a full *burqah*. These new rules were issued by the Ministry for the Promotion of Virtue and Suppression of Vice (PVSV), and compliance enforced by Saudi style religious police. Even the non-Pashtun Afghans had to comply.

The country under the Taliban became a haven for terrorist; it was recognized only by United Arab Emirates (UAE), Saudi Arabia and Pakistan.[274]

Al Qaeda, a radical Sunni Muslim organization was formed in the late 1980's to root out all foreign influence in Muslim countries. They run a stateless army of Muslim *jihadis,* planning suicide missions to accomplish their goals.[275] The 9/11 attacks were their most notable. The Taliban openly support Al Qaeda operatives. Following the 9/11 attacks, the U.S. and its allies made the following demands on the Taliban:

1. Arrest and hand over all Al Qaeda leaders including Osama bin Laden

2. Release all foreign nationals unjustly imprisoned

3. Protect journalists, aid workers and diplomats

4. Close all terrorist training camps

5. Hand over all terrorists

The Taliban never complied. The only country to recognize Taliban-ruled Afghanistan after the 9/11 attack was Pakistan, with ISI allegedly maintaining direct contact with the Taliban leaders to this day. Could ISI also provide shelter to the world's most wanted terrorist?

---

[274]"Taliban." *Wikipedia the free encyclopedia.* Wikipedia, The Free Encyclopedia, 22 Sept. 2010. Web. 22 Sept 2010. http://en.wikipedia.org/ wiki/Taliban

[275]"Al-Qaeda," *Wikipedia, The Free Encyclopedia.* Wikipedia, The Free Encyclopedia, 31 Oct. 2010. Web. I Nov. 2010

With the help of the U.S. and the coalition forces, the Northern Alliance was able to oust Taliban from Kabul in 2001 and re-instate a democratic government. Unfortunately, there is a resurgence of the Taliban, and life in Afghanistan remains plagued by road side bombs, suicide attacks and armed conflicts. Meanwhile, the military and civilian casualties keep rising. Who stands to benefit from a protracted war? Is there more than meets the eye?

An estimated 75 percent of the world's supply of opium comes from Afghanistan—over 4000 metric tons a year, worth $1.25 billion according to UN Office on Drugs and Crime (UNODC). Despite claims to an Islamic way of life, the Taliban ironically condone the farming of opium, because it is supposedly consumed only by the non-Muslim "infidels." Are there drug lords within the Taliban controlling events in the region? Could certain corrupt members of Pakistan's ISI also stand to gain from the opium trade? Could the regime in Afghanistan actually benefit from the opium trade? Do they all stand to gain from peace or protracted conflict in the region?[276]

Criminal Organizations

The international criminal organizations have their powerful grasp on the inner workings of practically every country in the world, especially if the country happens to be rich in natural

---

[276]Gretchen Peters -"How Opium Profits the Taliban." United States Institute of Peace, Washington DC. Aug. 2009. Web. 22 Sept 2010.
http://www.usip.org/files/resources/taliban_opium_1.pdf

resources and of strategic importance.[277] Major history-making events such as the downfall of the Soviet Union, the breakup of former Yugoslavia, and countless armed conflicts in various parts of the world are examples of how power-wielding groups of individuals carry out their agendas with the help of organized crime gangs, bypassing the protocols set by the UN. The funding of such activities is dependent on bank-laundered money, often made through illegal arms and drug deals. Those who may be viewed as threats or obstacles to the successful completion of the greed-driven missions are conveniently assassinated and their deaths made to look either accidental or natural. Despite many articles and books published by courageous investigative journalists, the mainstream media is alarmingly silent on such matters.[278] What is rather disturbing is that the criminal organizations may have reached even into the workings of modern Western democracies. Even more disturbing is that some countries have come to rely on such thugs to carry out their geopolitical goals. Can modern society hope for peace if organized crime is so intricately involved in global politics? Can it even win the war on drugs or the war on terror?

One region of the world that seems rife with tensions is the Indian sub-continent. It has been the center of greed-driven

---

[277]"Organized Crime." *Wikipedia, The Free Encyclopedia*. Wikipedia, The Free Encyclopedia, 17 July 2010. Web. 18 July 2010.
http://en.wikipedia.org/wiki/Organized_crime

[278]Daniel Estulin, *Shadow Masters: How Governments and Their Intelligence Agencies are Working with Drug Dealers and Terrorists for Mutual Benefit and Profit* (Walterville, OR: Trine Day, 2010). Print.

attention since the creation of the East India Trading Company in the seventeenth century. Plundering and pillage went on for two full centuries under various guises despite the actions of the well-intentioned British, who not only united the country into a cohesive nation but also left behind a legacy benefiting the nation even today. But, was there a greed-driven hidden agenda? The course of events makes one suspicious. At the time of independence in 1947, the country was partitioned along religious lines into three parts—a secular India, and Muslim West and East Pakistan (now Bangladesh). Perhaps the splintering was unavoidable. But could India's Partition and the continued tensions among the nations be created for the greed-driven geo-political goals of criminal elements that may have infiltrated the system worldwide? There has been enough bloodshed, rape and pillage already. Citizens of India and Pakistan who have so much in common need to lobby hard for peace. The elected leaders of both sides need to exercise restraint and give peace a chance. This will take ignoring the recurring instigations, and, above all, remaining ever mindful of the greedy vultures circling overhead.

Powerful Organizations

Some powerful organizations are worthy of a brief mention. Their membership and business are often not public knowledge, yet their members hold a lot of sway on world leaders and events. They are the following:

◊   The Council on Foreign Relations (CFR)

◊   OPEC

◊   Rendon Group

◊ The Illuminati (New World Order)

◊ Skull and Bones

◊ The Bilderberg Group

◊ Freemasonry

◊ The Unification Church of the Rev. Sun Myung Moon

◊ Trilateral Commission

These organizations perhaps have the best brains and intentions, and offer invaluable advice to the decision makers worldwide. However, could the democratically elected world leaders become mere puppets of such powerful organizations? Or, could personal bias or bigotry of the most vocal and power-wielding members of the organizations affect the inner workings of their groups? Could select members, driven by personal greed or hidden agendas, hijack the groups' benevolence? Or, that personal grudges and disagreements become a contest of wills, and the world becomes their chess board, and humans the chess pieces? What is the ethnicity of the members? Are there representatives from all corners of the world? How many of their members are women?

One can only hope that each and every member is a benevolent philanthropist and free of bias. Hopefully, they have enough checks and balances to prevent adverse results in the world, and that careful attention to detail is an integral part of their modus operandi. Today, such attention is more critical when political corruption, suicide bombings, and global terrorism plague and threaten modern civilization. If not, the slightest oversight and misstep on their part could have far reaching effects and repercussions.

If such powerful organizations are dedicated to improving life on the planet, then what is the purpose of secrecy that shrouds some of them? Does the secrecy allow its members to say what they want off the record? Does this not tacitly condone hypocrisy? Wouldn't transparency bring more respect for the organizations and its members, and win the support and co-operation of average citizens?

At a minimum, maybe these organizations ought to redefine or revisit their vision, mission, and values to suit the changing modern world so that civilized people do not live in constant fear. Whatever their modus operandi, here are some issues that could be addressed to promote peace and harmony for a unified world:

◊ Eliminate world hunger without promoting monopolies and oligarchies

◊ Promote human rights that include racial and gender equality

◊ Promote free speech and democracy

◊ Promote a meaningful education for all

◊ Offer gainful employment and dignity of labor to every willing person

◊ Promote religious, cultural, and racial harmony; not stopping at mere tolerance

◊ Promote free trade without interference by special interest groups driven purely by unadulterated greed

◊ Promote fair and responsible fiscal and monetary policies around the world

◊ Use diplomacy, incentives and disincentives to move people towards a peaceful unified world

◊ Work towards disarmament and peace

". . . Government of the people, by the people, for the people shall not perish from the earth."

– Abraham Lincoln (1809–1865)

Chapter 9
Power and Privilege in the Media and Entertainment

People shouldn't expect the mass media to do investigative stories. That job belongs to the 'fringe' media.

– by an English-born American broadcast journalist and Anchor

Any dictator would admire the uniformity and obedience of the U.S. media.

– Noam Chomsky (born in 1928)
American political activist and philosopher;
Professor Emeritus of Linguistics at the
Massachusetts Institute of Technology (MIT)

Who wields the power over what is seen on screens, printed in magazines and newspapers, or heard on radios? Given the vast and diverse industries involved—and their global scope—one would imagine the number of power-wielding entities in the industry too high to count.

Wrong. The power is mostly concentrated in fewer than ten such entities worldwide. Could only a handful of powerful people control the news reporters and news readers on TV and radio, as well as what appears in magazines and newspapers? Deregulation of the industry throughout the world in the 1980s, at the behest of the International Monetary Fund (IMF) and the U.S. government, privatization of the media and communications led to the demise of local, national and regional service providers. In its stead, there are nine big corporations and their subsidiaries in the industry worldwide.[279, 280]

Corporatization of the media world may be having undesired consequences.

Global Monopolies

Below are the multinational corporations that enjoy a global oligarchy:

TIME-WARNER-TURNER: It is the owner of or has significant financial interest in over a dozen TV stations that capture 25 percent of the American audience. It has the largest cable network with a 22 percent market share; its cable channels include CNN, Headline News, TNT, HBO, and Cinemax. It also provides U.S. satellite service through PrimeStar. It owns Warner Brothers and New Line Cinema studios, a chain of movie theaters, two dozen magazines including *Time*, *People*, and *Sports Illustrated*, as well as comics such as Superman and Batman. It also owns Time-Life Books—the second largest book publishing business in the world, Warner Music Group and professional sports teams.

DISNEY: It is the owner of, or has financial interest in ten U.S. television stations and 20 radio stations, including ABC Disney channels, ESPN, A&E, History channels. It

---

[279]Robert W. McChesney, *Corporate Media and the Threat to Democracy* (New York: Seven Stories Press and Open Media, 1997). Print.

[280]Melissa Rossi, *What Every American Should Know About Who's Really Running the World – The People, Corporations, Organizations That Control Our Future*; Penguin Group USA 2005. Print.

has interests in interactive TV with telephone companies (Americast), publishing magazines, newspapers, books and recorded music, and theme parks.

BERTELSMANN: owns or has financial interest in German, British, French, and Dutch TV channels, over 30 radio stations in Europe, more than 100 magazines, and over 40 book publishing houses producing works in the German, French and English languages.

VIACOM: owns or has significant financial interest in cable TV, including MTV, Showtime, Nickelodeon, VH1, and Comedy Central (with Time-Warner); in film and video productions including Paramount Pictures and movie theater, United Cinemas International, one of the largest in the world; in Blockbuster Video and Music Stores—the world's largest; and book publishers including Simon and Schuster, MacMillan and Scribners; and theme parks.

NEWS CORPORATION: owns, or has significant financial interest in, U.S. Fox network, which includes FOX News, as well as over 20 U.S. TV channels that reach 40 percent of U.S. households; satellite services under Sky Broadcasting in Europe, Asia and Latin America; movie, TV and video productions including Twentieth Century Fox; over 130 newspapers worldwide (one of the largest market shares in the world), including the *London Times*, two dozen magazines including *TV Guide*; book publishing including Harper-Collins; and sports teams. The founder, Chairman and CEO of the company has been at the center of the phone hacking scandal in the UK. To read how governments are controlled: http://www.guardian.co.uk/commentisfree/2012/apr/28/news-corporation-governments

TCI: (Telecommunications, Inc.): has significant interests in TV channels including Discovery, Fox Sports Net, Black

Entertainment TV, Court TV and the Home Shopping Network. It is also a major shareholder in Time-Warner.

GENERAL ELECTRIC: owns NBC, which owns or has financial interest in U.S. television and radio stations, including CNBC, MSNBC and A&E.

SONY: (owner of Columbia and TriStar Pictures): has major financial interest in the music industry (CBS records), TV, and video productions.

SEAGRAM: owns Universal (formerly MCA). Also owns fifteen percent of Time-Warner.

What is wrong with the above scenario? Certainly, not all that is presented is bad for humanity. In fact, these multinational corporations promote art and music, advance peace and harmony, promote equality and even stimulate critical thinking. Furthermore, they are likely to wield substantial power to reveal the truth even in the face of powerful adversarial forces. But profits receive priority in the corporate world. And profits in the media and entertainment world come from advertising. Would a media company want to offend a powerful multinational corporation that advertises during prime-time television or places full-page advertisements in its newspapers and magazines? Do conflicts of interest ever affect the administrative decisions? How much freedom do the reporters and investigative journalists really have in this oligarchy?

The world is full of diverse ethnic groups. Consequently, there are as many accents of English as there are races. There are varied accents of the language within the U.S. alone. Yet, one hears only a few select accents on radio and television. Do all news readers, announcers, and reporters go to the same select schools? Do budding journalists strive to rid themselves of their unique characteristics of speech and adopt the prevailing successful accents? Or, do only select groups of people make it in the media world?

The UK-based British Broadcasting Corporation (BBC) and the Qatar-based *Al Jazeera* claim to be fair and balanced broadcasting organizations compared to others in the world. They both claim to be independent of interference from their respective heads of state or other political leaders. Is there validity to their claim?

The BBC was started under a Royal Charter in 1927. In its 2006 copy of the Charter on broadcasting, it states in clause 6 (1) that the BBC shall be independent. But, in clause 6(2) it states: "Paragraph 6(1) is subject to any provision made by or under this Charter or any Framework, Agreement or otherwise by law.[281] Furthermore, BBC is governed both by a Trust and an Executive Board. But, all members of the Trust are appointed. And, more importantly, the Chairman of the Board is appointed by the Trust. Could there be an Old Boys' Club or conflict of interest in such a process? And, could board members and trustees be former government officials or executives of multinational corporations with a vested interest?

---

[281]Royal Charter for the Continuance of the British Broadcasting Corporation, October 2006. Web. 22 Aug 2010. http://www.bbc.co.uk/bbctrust/assets/files/pdf/about/how_we_govern/charter.pdf

Al Jazeera was started in 1996 with a loan of US$137 million from the Emir of Qatar, after the Saudi BBC office was closed due to censorship by the Saudi Arabian government. Since then it has continued to depend on funding from the Emir. The Chairman of the company is a cousin of the Emir. The network has strived to present a balanced view point on world events. But, is *Al Jazeera* likely to broadcast anything that may offend the Emir or the Royal families of the region— even if it were true? Is it likely to speak out against fanatic and powerful Imams?[282]

In the media world, it is more of a concern when the big corporations are always poised to buy out competition in the industry. Thus, over time, could mergers and acquisitions eliminate competition throughout the world, making citizens even more helpless against the powerful multinational corporations? Or, worse still, rendered helpless to fight the megalomaniacs and the misguided, power-hungry evildoers like Hitler and Stalin?

⬜ ⬜ ⬜

So is it possible that news reports may be tweaked, some news completely suppressed, some movies never distributed, some books never published? Is investigative journalism dying? Is free press going to become a thing of the past for the main-

---

[282]Aljazeera. *Wikipedia, The Free Encyclopedia.* Wikipedia, The Free Encyclopedia. Web. 22 Aug 2010. http://en.wikipedia.org/wiki/Aljazeera

stream media? Could average citizens turn to unconventional modes of acquiring accurate information? Are they likely to get unadulterated news, and share their views on social media? Should abusers of the world, including dictators, beware?

Nothing strengthens authority as much as silence.
– Leonardo da Vinci (1452–1519)
Italian painter, sculptor, architect, and writer

All that is necessary for the triumph of evil is for good men [or good women] to do nothing.
– Edmund Burke (1729–1797)
Anglo-Irish statesman, author and political theorist, and member of the British House of Commons

Chapter 10
Power and Privilege of Ethnicity

Ethnicity can be defined by a host of factors including the country of birth, family history, ancestry, language, religion, culture or even physical appearance. It is not uncommon for the dominant and powerful ethnic group in any given region of the world to view other group(s) as inferior, even subhuman at times.

Among the factors that define ethnicity, the birthplace of an individual is perhaps the most significant. The importance of birthplace is a societal concept. After one's birth date, the birthplace, especially the country of birth, is the most important detail of the person. It is always mentioned prominently in all the important documents such as birth certificates and passports. Why is the place of birth so important? Does birthplace put some individuals at an advantage and others at a disadvantage?

Consider this. The mere chance, or call it sheer luck, of being born in a Western European or North American nation brings to the fortunate individual lifelong travel privileges that are denied to those born in sub-Saharan Africa or parts of Asia. The privilege of birth in North America or Western Europe also brings respectful and civil treatment from everybody, especially the immigration officials at ports of entry. Those not as fortunate suffer a lifelong stigma—inability to travel freely in the modern affluent world, and treatment resembling that accorded to the lepers of the Biblical era.

Travel restrictions across international borders are understandable. The cost of providing essential services to illegal aliens falls on the tax payers of the host country. The illegals work for cash in the informal sectors well below the radar screens. They also steal jobs from the natives by working for less money and cause unemployment. The problem of illegal immigration from poor third-world nations flooding the workforce in the affluent host countries could conceivably throw the economy into a tailspin and cause a recession. But most aliens take jobs that the natives prefer not to. And, their cheap labor make things more affordable for citizens. How could the contribution by such workers be duly recognized and accounted for? How many illegal aliens are forced into crime in order to survive? How can the modern world address this problem? Perhaps it may be wise for the nations of the world to revisit and redesign the global economy and work towards fair wages and global work permits as a start.

Discriminatory restrictions on citizens have historically been imposed within a country based on ethnicity. For example, the blacks in the U.S. could not use services at gas stations, barber shops, public drinking fountains, restrooms, hotels and restaurants up until the passage of the Civil Rights Act in 1964.[283] They depended on the *Negro Motorist Green Book,* a directory that listed businesses where blacks were not subjected to indignities.

The most recent example of such discrimination was the travel restriction imposed upon the Muslim Uighur Chinese before

---

[283]Celia McGee. "The Open Road Wasn't Quite Open to All." *The New York Times.* The New York Times, 22 Aug 2010. Web. 15 Sept 2010. http://www.nytimes.com/2010/08/23/books/23green.html

and during the 2008 Olympic Games.[284] The short-term gain from such treatment of Muslim Chinese was at the expense of long-term trust and harmony. Would such shortsighted treatment of citizens suppress or encourage terrorism in the long run?

Another relatively benign form of ethnic bias manifests in the real estate business in some parts of the world. The undesirable ethnicities are barred from owning or renting homes, building places of worship or owning commercial spaces in certain neighborhoods. For example, in India, meat-eating Muslims cannot buy or rent property in neighborhoods with a vegetarian majority. In the U.S., people of color suffer similar discrimination. Such discriminatory practices were brazen in the U.S. up until the mid-1900s. The exclusion of blacks from buying a home in Levittown, Pennsylvania, is a case in point.[285] Today the practice is illegal since the passage of the Fair Housing Act of 1968. But do real estate agents continue to scare home owners of impending influx of undesirable race in their neighborhoods, or try to preserve and encourage racial segregation? As recently as 2006, well-known real estate companies have had lawsuits brought against them for such racial "steering."[286]

---

[284]"Travel Restrictions for China Muslims." *Islam Online*. Islam Online, 31 July 2008. Web. 17 July 2010. http://www.islamonline.net/servlet/Satellite?c=Article_C&cid=1216208215783&pagename=Zone-English-News/NWELayout

[285]"Levittown, Pennsylvania." *Wikipedia, The Free Encyclopedia*. Wikipedia, The Free Encyclopedia, 12 July 2010. Web. 20 June 2010. http://en.wikipedia.org/wiki/Levittown,_Pennsylvania -20 June 2010 at 22:38.

[286]Racial steering. *Wikipedia, The Free Encyclopedia*. Wikipedia, The Free Encyclopedia. 5 Oct 2010. Web. 20 Oct 2010. http://en.wikipedia.org/wiki/Racial_steering

Invasion and colonization of Asia, Australia, Africa and the Americas by European countries were the norm a few centuries ago. Often the indigenous populations suffered from epidemics, death in large numbers, economic devastation, and social deprivation not only from gross negligence, but also by systematic abuse of power by the settlers.

The transportation of millions of blacks from Africa to serve as slaves in the U.S. is a glaring example of abuse of power by privileged ethnic groups of the times. The U.S. slave trade began in the Sixteenth Century; it was legalized in the Seventeenth Century by Massachusetts, Connecticut, Virginia, Maryland, New York and New Jersey. By 1860 there were four million slaves in the country. The trade lasted for three centuries, finally ending in 1865.[287]

The most malignant form of ethnic bias manifests as ethnic cleansing and genocide. The powerful ethnic group subjugates the "inferior" group(s) and resorts to systematic extermination. Some [randomly selected] examples of ethnic cleansing and genocides that have occurred in the past few centuries in various parts of the world include the following:

◊   In Turkey, under the Ottoman Empire, against the Armenians, the Assyrians, the Kurds, and the Greeks

◊   In Ireland, against the Irish by British rulers (in the form of mass starvation—the great Irish famine)

◊   In North America, against the Native Americans by European settlers

---

[287]History of Slavery. *Wikipedia, The Free Encyclopedia*. Wikipedia, The Free Encyclopedia. 24 Oct 2010. Web. 24 Oct 2010.
http://en.wikipedia.org/wiki/History_of_slavery#North_America

◊ In Australia, against the Aborigines by European settlers

◊ In the Philippines, against the Filipinos by Americans

◊ In German Southwest Africa, against the Herero and Nama populations by the German settlers

◊ In Czarist Russia, against the indigenous people of west Caucasus, the Circassian (Muhajirs)

◊ In the Soviet Union, against the Ukranians (Holodomor—Murder by Hunger)

◊ In Brazil, India, and northern China—death by mass hunger caused by the willfully negligent policies of the late Victorian era British rule during the famines of the Nineteenth Century while the food was shipped for profits to feed Europe.

◊ In Croatia, against the Serbs, the Jews, and the Romany under the Ustashe regime

◊ In Nazi Germany and occupied territories, against the Jews, Jehovah's witnesses, Poles, Russians, Ukrainians, Belarusians, Serbs, Romany, mentally ill, and "sexual devants." [288, 289]

Even though the UN first made efforts in 1948, with the promulgation of the Convention on the Prevention and Punishment of the Crime of Genocide (CPPCG), which later became an international law, genocides have continued unabated.

---

[288]"Ethnic Cleansing." *Wikipedia, The Free Encyclopedia.* Wikipedia, The Free Encyclopedia, 16 July 2010. Web. 18 July 2010. http://en.wikipedia.org/wiki/Ethnic_cleansing

[289]Mike Davis, *"Late Victorian Holocausts - El Nino Famines and the Making of the Third World."* London, Verso, 2002. Print.

Below is a table listing countries where genocides have taken place since then:[290]

Country	Year genocide began	Approximate duration
Sudan	1956	16 years
China	1959	9 months
South Vietnam	1965	10 years
Iraq	1963	12 years
Algeria	1962	5 months
Rwanda	1963	6 months
Congo-Kinshasa	1964	11 months
Burundi	1965	8 months
Indonesia	1965	8 months
China	1966	9 years
Guatemala	1978	18 years
East Pakistan	1971	9 months
Uganda	1972	7 years
Philippines	1972	4 years
Pakistan	1973	4 years
Chile	1973	3 years
Mexico	1968	2 years
Angola	1975	26 years
Cambodia	1975	17 years
Indonesia	1975	17 years
Argentina	1976	4 years
Ethiopia	1976	3 years
Congo-Kinshasa	1977	2 years
Afghanistan	1978	14 years
Burma	1978	11 months
El Salvador	1980	9 years
Uganda	1980	5 years
Syria	1981	1 year
Iran 1981	1981	11 years
Sudan	1983	27 years and on-going
Iraq	1988	3 years
Somalia	1988	3 years
Bosnia	1992	3 years
Burundi	1993	2 years
Rwanda	1994	3 months
Serbia	1998	1 year
Sri Lanka	1983	26 years

[290]"Genocides in History." *Wikipedia, The Free Encyclopedia.* Wikipedia, The Free Encyclopedia, 17 July 2010. Web. 18 July 2010.
http://en.wikipedia.org/wiki/Genocides_in_history

These mass murders have led to the extermination of over 18 million people in the last half a century alone.

What is the point of listing these mass murders and their duration here and not as an appendix? How many people who read or watch the news every day remember reading or hearing about these mass murders taking place? How many brushed aside their news quickly? Maybe people have become desensitized by the horrors they constantly read about and see on the screens every day. Maybe some still think it is survival of the fittest and a natural selection process. But, could survivors of genocides turn into vengeful, fierce and unrelenting fighters of tomorrow?

No other genocide is more publicized than the one at the behest of the Nazis. Despite countless reports and graphic pictures, including detailed testimony by survivors, there are people who still deny the extermination of millions of innocent civilians. Such an attitude is socially irresponsible and morally bankrupt.

It was not until June of 1998 that the UN General Assembly established the International Criminal Court (ICC) at The Hague to try perpetrators of war crimes and crimes against humanity.[291] But, the ICC can only prosecute crimes committed since 2002.[292]

---

[291]"International Criminal Court." *Wikipedia, The Free Encyclopedia.* Wikipedia, The Free Encyclopedia, 18 July 2010. Web. 18 July 2010. http://en.wikipedia.org/wiki/International_Criminal_Court

[292]Rome Statute of the International Criminal Court.UN.1999-2003. Web. 17 July 2010 http://www.un.org/law/icc/index.html; http://www.icc-cpi.int/Menus/ICC/About+the+Court/

One way to empower the ICC in putting an end to future genocides would be to declare the *funding* of such mass killings, as well as the *supplying of weapons* to areas of conflict, as abetting in crimes against humanity. Why? Consider the fact that somebody, somewhere (usually far away), stands to gain in the long run from fueling armed conflicts. But then, would the powerful countries manufacturing and supplying the weapons ratify such a UN treaty?

One of the most glaring examples of abuse of male power of one ethnic group over another is the war-related rape of women of the vanquished by victorious armies. Rapes during wartime and genocidal rape have been occurring all throughout history, and yet there is a disturbing absence of even a passing mention in history books. In 1993, Catharine Mackinnon aptly described the plight of women in Bosnia-Herzegovina:

> *This is not rape out of control. It is rape under*
> *control. It is also rape unto death, rape as massacre,*
> *rape to kill and to make you leave your home and*
> *never want to go back. It is rape to be seen and heard*
> *and watched and told to others: rape as spectacle. It*
> *is rape to drive a wedge through a community, to*
> *shatter a society, to destroy a people. It is rape as*
> *genocide [. . .] murder as the ultimate sexual act*
> *[. . .] rape as ethnic expansion through forced*
> *reproduction . . .* [293]

---

[293] *Century of Genocide.* Century of Genocide, 2008. Web. 17 July 2010. http://centuryofgenocide.com/exhibition/page47/page1/page1.html

At a meeting hosted by the women faculty of the Harvard Law School in Boston, Massachusetts, female victims from all the warring ethnic groups of the former Yugoslavia described the horrors they suffered. It came as no surprise to see that the women from the various warring groups harbored little or no hatred toward each other. Thanks to the efforts of the women faculty of the Harvard Law School, the ICC included genocidal rape as a crime against humanity.

However, genocidal rape goes on unabated despite the ICC.[294] In Congo, there has been an ongoing rape epidemic since 2007, and it continues unabated in 2010. Doctors there have been treating countless women and girls who have been "butchered inside and out" with bayonets and chunks of wood, "destroying their digestive and reproductive organs beyond repair."[295]

There is a flicker of hope in this seemingly endless dark and sinister tunnel of history. After handing down the verdict on the first trial of crime against humanity in Rwanda, ICC's presiding judge, a Tamil South African woman, Navanethem Pillay, said in a statement after the verdict:

---

[294] *A New UN Voice Calls for Criminalizing Conflict Rape.* Barbara Crossette, September 10, 2010. The Nation. Web. 10 Sept 2010.
http://www.thenation.com/article/154624/new-un-voice-calls-criminalizing-conflict-rape

[295] Jeffrey Gettleman. "Rape Epidemic Raises Trauma of Congo War." *NY Times.* October 7 2007. Web. Sept 10 2010.
http://www.nytimes.com/2007/10/07/world/africa/07congo.html?pagewanted=all

From time immemorial, rape has been regarded as spoils of war. Now it will be considered a war crime. We want to send out a strong message that rape is no longer a trophy of war.[296]

Perhaps the world can hope for true equality and real justice for all in the future.

What connects two thousand years of genocide? Too much power in too few hands.

— Simon Wiesenthal (1908–2005)
Austrian Jewish engineer and Holocaust survivor

I believe all suffering is caused by ignorance. People inflict pain on others in the selfish pursuit of their happiness or satisfaction. . .

— His Holiness the Dalai Lama

---

[296]"International Criminal Tribunal for Rwanda." *Wikipedia, The Free Encyclopedia.* Wikipedia, The Free Encyclopedia, 3 July 2010. Web. 18 July 2010.
http://en.wikipedia.org/wiki/International_Criminal_Tribunal_for_Rwanda

Chapter 11
Power and Privilege of Weapons of War

The privilege to make weapons, especially weapons of mass destruction (WMDs), has often been the subject of debate, especially at the United Nations (UN). It seems as though the UN has an innate authority to determine which nation can have the privilege of making or stockpiling such weapons. Some questions seem worthy of note. To whom does the UN grant that privilege? Does the privilege depend on the *veto* power any given nation wields in the UN? Does the UN buckle under pressure from nations that already have such weapons? Does the privilege of stockpiling them have anything to do with the promotion of world peace? Do some nations secretly enjoy the privilege? And once the nation is privileged to have WMDs, is this privilege abused in the name of deterrence; even threatening adversarial nations? Is the death of thousands of innocent civilians—men, women and children, from WMDs merely collateral damage not worthy of note?

An estimated U.S. $1 trillion [$1,000,000,000,000] are spent on military expenditures worldwide (2 percent of World GDP).[297] The sales of the 100 large arms-producing companies amounted

---

[297] *Global Issues*. Global Issues, 1998-2010. Web. 17 July 2010. www.globalissues.org

to an estimated $315 billion worth in 2006 alone.[298] The top three military equipment and arms manufacturing and exporting nations in the world are the U.S. with 15 companies devoted to military, China with 10 and Russia with 14 such companies.[299]

What could the UN do to curtail the arms race? The weapons industry must have a similar operating model to any other industry. Without money precious little can be achieved. Both small and large weapons manufacturers require funds for research and development, initial capital expenditure, purchase of raw materials and parts, as well as operating costs; they require a distribution and delivery system and last, but not least, funds to be paid by end users. The amount of money exchanging hands would be quite substantial. Furthermore, the money transactions for arms delivery to rogue nations or into regions of conflict are likely to be considerably higher. Some questions may be worth considering. Who funds the entire process from research and development to the end users? If the world were serious about putting an end to armed conflicts, the member nations of the UN could follow the money trail of the weapons trade.

After the September 11 terrorist attacks, the UN and all member nations successfully united to follow the money trail of terrorist groups, and stop all transactions of terrorist cells throughout

---

[298]*SIPRI.* Stockholm International Peace Research Institute, 2010. Web. 17 July 2010. http://www.sipri.org

[299]"Major Arms Industry Corporations by Nation." *Wikipedia, The Free Encyclopedia.* Wikipedia, The Free Encyclopedia, 11 July 2010. Web. 18 July 2010.
http://en.wikipedia.org/wiki/Major_arms_industry_ corporations_ by_nation

the world. What holds them back from doing the same for the weapons trade to achieve world peace? But, will the powerful members of the UN who stand to benefit from the weapons' trade give peace a chance?

In 1961, President Dwight Eisenhower in his farewell address to the Nation warned Americans thus:

> *We must guard against the acquisition of unwarranted influence whether sought or unsought; we must guard against the rise of the military industrial complex. The potential for the disastrous rise of misplaced power exists and will persist.*[300]

Today there seems to be a *military-industrial-media-academic* complex. Facts seem suppressed and truths distorted to serve a select few.

Do defense contractors wield considerable power and influence over elected leaders of the world? Is the threat of being dragged into unjustified wars real? The possibility is quite disturbing.

It is even more disturbing to see a mad rush to buy the stocks of publicly traded companies that have sizable defense contracts. The stocks of such companies often skyrocket at the outset of a war. Does this not imply that average citizens in the free market economy are exercising their privilege by investing money indirectly in the pain and suffering of innocent civilians, death and destruction in the war zones? Wouldn't all humanity and all life on this planet be better served by *investing in peace*?

---

[300] *"Why We Fight"* produced and directed by Eugene Jarecki, Sony Pictures Classics Release -2006. Film.

On May 20, 2010, Vision of Humanity's website posted an article entitled, "Why We Should Invest in Peace."[301] Below are a few worthy observations contained in the article:

◊ Wars are no longer economically viable.

◊ Nations with functioning governments, high levels of education, freedom of the press, low levels of corruption, and good relations with their neighboring states are more likely to be peaceful. In the absence of these key ingredients, elections become catalysts for violence

◊ Violence suppresses economic activity

◊ The annual economic cost of lost peace is U.S $7.2 trillion [$7,200,000,000,000]

◊ Global Peace Index (GPI) ranks nations of the world by their peacefulness. Nations with high GPI display tolerance and respect for human rights, enjoy freedom of the press, do not believe that they are superior to others, and believe that the military use should be limited and internationally sanctioned

◊ Survival of society in the 21st century and beyond depends on peace.[302]

---

[301]Steve Killelea and Camilla Schippa, "Why We Should Invest in Peace," *Economics and Peace*. 20 May 2010. Web. 20 Oct 2010.
http://www.visionofhumanity.org/info-center/vision-of-humanity-themes/economics-and-peace/invest-in-peace/

[302]"Global Peace Index," *Wikipedia, The Free Encyclopedia*. Wikipedia, The Free Encyclopedia. 23 Oct 2010. Web. 24 Oct 2010.
http://en.wikipedia.org/wiki/Global_Peace_Index

Below is a list of selected nations and their GPI:

Countries	Rank among 149
New Zealand	1
Japan	3
Sweden	10
Canada	14
Switzerland	18
Australia	19
U.K.	31
China	80
United States	85
India	128
Russian Federation	143
Israel	144
Afghanistan, Somalia and Iraq	Last three

For a full list please visit the website:

http://www.visionofhumanity.org/gpi-data/#/2010/scor.

Increased awareness of national GPI ranking could help people invest in peace, harmony, human rights, social justice and progress. Perhaps there ought to be a Peace Index based on race and religion. A visit to the website of the Australia-based organization, Institute for Economics and Peace may be a good start:

http://www.economicsandpeace.org/AboutUs

Better than a thousand hollow words, is one word that brings peace.

— The Buddha (563–483 BCE)

Spiritual teacher from ancient
India who founded Buddhism

Make better choices to create the kind of future in which you wish to live.

— Steve Killelea [born 1949]

Founder of Institute for Economics and Peace
and creator of GPI

When I despair, I remember that all through history the way of truth and love has always won. There have been tyrants and murderers and for a time they seem invincible but in the end, they always fall—think of it, ALWAYS!

— Mahatma Gandhi

Peace is not merely a distant goal that we seek, but a means by which we arrive at that goal.

— Martin Luther King, Jr. (1929–1968)

American Minister and leader of the
Civil Rights Movement that challenged
the segregation laws of the South

You cannot shake hands with a clenched fist.

— Indira Gandhi (1917–1984)

Indian Prime Minister 1966–77 and 1980–84

Conclusion

Power and privilege are seductive forces. To the privileged comes power; with power come privileges. The two are often camouflaged in the hands of the unscrupulous abusers. Their abuses lead to mass deception, corruption, injustice, exploitation, cruelty to others, and large-scale death and destruction. They do so either to satisfy their greed for material things or a morbid appetite for exercising authority.

Whether power is bestowed upon individuals or acquired with fierce and single-minded devotion, their abuses are harmful to society. Some individuals promote their powerful and privileged status by surrounding themselves by like-minded cronies. Such people must be recognized, carefully watched and curtailed—they lurk everywhere. Their abuses are often disguised as family values, culture, tradition, religion, progress, patriotism and justice.

How can such abuses be stopped? At the family level, abusive behavior must be nipped in the bud. If not, today's abused will become the abusers of tomorrow. The problem must be dealt with using the help of other family members, family counseling, community support and the law.

At the institutional level, tackling abuses may be a bit more challenging. Often the abusers are protected by elaborate infrastructure, while the abused are often weak and vulnerable. In such instances, the abused must use their collective strength to expose the perpetrators. Personality traits, motives and hidden agendas of abusive individuals must be recognized. Using the strength in numbers, a unified effort in exposing and condemning their abuses must be made without fear. Only then such individuals can be eliminated from their positions of power and authority before they damage the institutions and society.

At the national and international level, citizens must remain particularly mindful of the insatiable appetite for power and privilege of appointed and elected leaders alike. They may band together to promote their privileges at the expense of average citizens.

In medieval times, abuse of power by leaders not only led to wars, but also enslaving of entire races, including genocidal rapes that have always been glossed over in history books. Today the abuses are often disguised in a web of deception and corruption. Compared to the bloody wars of the past the abuses of today are rather insidious. They take the form of blockades and economic sanctions cloaked in righteousness, but serving the geopolitical goals of the powerful. Such tactics of modern economic warfare are often overt, but are sometimes covert.[303] They even come disguised as aid—the price often too dear to pay. Consequently, such abuses result in some form of ethnic cleansing, slow destruction, injustice, exploitation and cruelty toward large segments of life on earth.

---

[303]John Perkins, *"Confessions of an Economic Hit Man,"* USA, First Plume Printing. 2006. Print.

Why isn't the abuse of power, especially at the expense of vast segments of humanity, declared a sin or a crime, and rooted out, especially when most humans believe in benevolence and empathy? Is this failure because people are too busy making ends meet, leaving little time to keep track of the abuses? Or, is there a dearth of accurate information?

It was not until 2002 that the International Criminal Court (ICC) was able to prosecute abusive leaders for genocide, crimes against humanity, and war crimes.[304] However, the ICC can only step in if the national courts fail to address such crimes. No respectable nation is likely to admit to the failure of its courts. Besides, courts, judges, and rulings can be bought by the powerful and the privileged of society almost anywhere. And, will ICC ever consider economic warfare that causes widespread suffering and displacement a crime against humanity? Is that why the most economically powerful nations have not yet ratified the ICC treaty?

　　　　　口　口　口

If modern civilization is to survive then it is time for individuals, both victims and perpetrators alike, in every part of the world, to think of the long-term consequences of abuses perpetrated today. The most important first step would be for people to resurrect their conscience and readjust the moral compass. Doing so will at least eliminate indoctrination and brainwashing.

---

[304]"International Criminal Court." *Wikipedia, The Free Encyclopedia.* Wikipedia, The Free Encyclopedia, 18 July 2010. Web. 18 July 2010. http://en.wikipedia.org/wiki/International_Criminal_Court

Such inner awakening is even more important for the abusers to consider. It will help eliminate the unscrupulous, amoral and greed-driven abuse of power and privilege.

It is time for all family elders, educators, executives, religious leaders, officers of the government, drug lords, judges, and elected officials as well as self-appointed leaders all over the world to do some soul-searching and become responsible planetary citizens. There is no escape-hatch to paradise and no personal salvation for anyone at the expense of others, the environment or world peace. After all, humans remain but mere mortals.

List of the current heirs apparent in the world:

◊ Bahrain: HRH Crown Prince Salman bin Hamad bin Isa Al Khalifa
◊ Belgium: HRH Prince Philippe, Duke of Brabant
◊ Brunei: HRH Crown Prince Al-Muhtadee Billah
◊ Denmark: HRH Crown Prince Frederik
◊ Dubai: Sheikh Hamdan bin Mohammed bin Rashid al Maktoum
◊ Japan: HIH Crown Prince Naruhito
◊ Kuwait: HRH Crown Prince Nawaf Al-Ahmad
◊ Al-Jaber Al-Sabah
◊ Lesotho: HRH Prince Lerotholi Seeiso
◊ Liechtenstein: HSH Prince Alois
◊ Luxembourg: HRH Hereditary Grand Duke Guillaume
◊ Morocco: HRH Crown Prince Moulay Hassan
◊ Netherlands: HRH Prince Willem-Alexander, Prince of Orange
◊ Norway: HRH Crown Prince Haakon
◊ Qatar: HRH Sheikh Tamim Bin Hamad Al Thani
◊ Saudi Arabia: HRH Crown Prince Sultan bin Abdul Aziz al-Saud
◊ Spain: HRH Prince Felipe, Prince of Asturias
◊ Thailand: HRH Crown Prince Maha Vajiralongkorn
◊ UK and sixteen thrones of the Commonwealth realms, *i.e.*, 16 sovereign states within the Commonwealth of Nations including Canada, Australia, New Zealand, Jamaica, Barbados, the Bahamas, Grenada, Papua New Guinea, the Solomon Islands, Tuvalu, Saint Lucia, Saint Vincent and the Grenadines, Belize, Antigua and Barbuda, and Saint Kitts and Nevis: HRH Prince Charles, Prince of Wales

List of organizations that help women:

Global:

◊ www.americansforunfpa.org supports UN Population Fund

◊ www.amddprogram.org focuses on maternal health (Averting Maternal Death and Disability)

◊ www.engenderhealth.org focuses on reproductive health

◊ www.equalitynow.org works against sex trade and gender oppression

◊ www.familycareintl.org focuses on maternal health

◊ www.globalfundforwomen.org. helps women's groups in poor countries

◊ www.thp.org focuses on empowering women and girls to end world hunger

◊ www.icrw.org supports women in economic development (International Center for Research on Women)

◊ www.pathfind.org supports reproductive health of women

◊ www.sharedhope.org fights sex trafficking

◊ www.thegirlfund.org works on the education, healthcare and protection from violence

◊ www.vitalvoices.org fights against trafficking

◊ www.womenforwomen.org connects women from poor countries and regions of conflict

◊ www.womenscampaigninternational.org dedicated to promote women's participation in political processes and governments

◊ www.learningpartnership.org supports women's empowerment and leadership

◊ www.womensrefugeecommission.org focuses on women refugees and children

◊ www.womensworldbanking.org focuses on micro-financing that assists women

Asia:

◊ www.apneaap.org fights against sex slavery in India

◊ www.cambodiaschools.com fights trafficking and supports education of girls

◊ www.penniesforpeace.org provides education of girls in Pakistan and Afghanistan

◊ www.sewa.org supports and educates women to be financially independent

Africa:

◊ www.canfed.org supports schooling for girls

Latin America:

◊ www.promujer.org supports women in Latin America

Alumni of London School of Economics who became Heads of State:

1. Barbados – The Rt Hon Errol Walton Barrow – Prime Minister
2. Bulgaria – Sergey Stanishev – Prime Minister
3. Canada –
   a. Rt Hon Pierre Trudeau – Prime Minister
   b. The Rt Hon Kim Campbell – Prime Minister
   c. Jacques Parizeau – Premier of Quebec
4. China – Yang Jiechi – Tenth foreign Minister of the People's Republic of China
5. Colombia – Dr. Pumarejo Alfonso López – President
6. Costa Rica – Oscar Rafael de Jesús Aria Sánchez – President
7. Denmark – HM Queen Margrethe II – Queen
8. Dominica – The Hon Dame Mary Eugenia Charles – Prime Minister
9. Fiji – The Rt Hon Ratu Sir Kamisese Mara – Prime Minister; President
10. Ghana –
    a. Dr. Kwame Nkrumah – First President
    b. Hon Dr. Hilla Limann – President
    c. John Atta Mills – President
11. Germany – Heinrich Bruning – Chancellor
12. Grenada – Maurice Bishop – Prime Minister
13. Greece –
    a. Dr. Constantine Simitis – Prime Minister
    b. George Papandreou – Prime Minister
14. Guyana – Forbes Burnham – President
15. India – Sri KR Narayanan – President
16. Israel – Moshe Sharett – Prime Minister
17. Italy – Professor Romano Prodi – Prime Minister; President of the European Commission

18. Jamaica –
    a. The Rt Hon Michael Manley – Prime Minister
    b. The Rt Hon P J Patterson – Prime Minister
19. Japan – Taro Aso – Prime Minister
20. Kenya
    a. Jomo Kenyatta – First President
    b. Mwai Kibaki – President
    c. Kiribati Anote Tong – President
21. Malaysia – Tuanku Jaafar – King
22. Mauritius –
    a. The Hon Sir Veerasamy Ringadoo – First President of Mauritius
    b. The Hon Dr. Navinchandra Ramgoolam – Prime Minister
23. Nepal – Sher Bahadur Deuba - Prime Minister
24. Panama – Harmodio Arias Madrid- President
25 Perú –
    a. Pedro Gerardo Beltran Espanto – Prime Minister
    b. Beatriz Merino Lucero – Prime Minister
26. Poland – Marek Belka – Prime Minister
27. Singapore – Goh Keng Swee – Minister of Finance, Minister   of Defense, Minister of Education, Deputy Prime Minister
28. St Lucia – The Hon John Compton – Premier; Prime Minister
29. Taiwan –
    a. Yu Kuo-Hwa – Premier
    b. Tsai Ing-wen – Vice-Premier
30. Thailand – Thanin Kraivichien – Prime Minister
31. Togo – Sylvanus Olympio – Prime Minister and President
32. UK – Lord Attlee – Prime Minister
33. U.S. – John F. Kennedy - President

Alumni of Oxford who became Heads of State:

1. Australia –
   a. John Gorton – Prime Minister
   b. Malcolm Fraser – Prime Minister
   c. Bob Hawke – Prime Minister
2. Barbados –
   a. Grantley Adams – Premier
   b. T.M.J. Adams – Prime Minister
3. Bhutan – J. K. N. Wangchuk – King
4. Botswana –
   a. Seretse Khama – King and later President
   b. Festus Mogae – President
5. Canada –
   a. John Napier Turner – Prime Minister
   b. Lester Bowles Pearson – Prime Minister
6. East Timor – Jose Ramos-Horta – Prime Minister
7. Fiji –
   a. Kamisese Mara – President
   b. Penaia Ganilau – President
8. Germany - Richard von Weizsacker – President
9. Ghana –
   a. John Kufuor – President
   b. Edward A. Addo – President
   c. Kofi Abrefa Busia – Prime Minister
10. Hungary – Viktor Orban – Prime Minister
11. India –
    a. Sarvepalli Radhakrishnan – President
    b. Manmohan Singh – Prime Minister
    c. Indira Gandhi – Prime Minister
12. Jamaica Norman Washington Manley – Prime Minister
13. Jordan – King Abdullah II

14. Malaysia –
    a. Sultan Ahemen Shaha – King/Sultan
    b. Tuanku Abdul Halim – King/Sultan
    c. Tuanku Jaafar – King
15. Malta –
    a. Dominic Mintoff – Prime Minister
    b. Andrew Bertie – Grand Master
16. Netherlands – William-II – King
17. Norway –
    a. King Harald – King
    b. Olav-V – King
18. Pakistan –
    a. Huseyn S. Suhrawardy – Prime Minister
    b. Zulfiqar Ali Bhutto – Prime Minister
    c. Benazir Bhutto – Prime Minister
    d. Wasim Sajjad – President
    e. Liakat ali Khan – Prime Minister
    f. Farooq Leghari – President
19. Peru – Pedro Pablo Kuczynski – Prime Minister
20. Siam – Vajiravhud – King
21. Sri Lanka – Solomon Bandranaike – Prime Minister
22. Thailand –
    a. Seni Pramoj – Prime Minister
    b. Kukrit Pramoj – Prime Minister
    c. Abhisit Vejjajiva – Prime Minister
23. Tonga – George Tupuo – King
24. Trinidad and Tobago –
    a. Eric Williams – Prime Minister
    b. A. N. R. Robinson – Prime Minister
25. UK – total of 25 Prime Ministers including William
    Gladstone, Herbert Asquith, Clement Attlee, Harold
    Macmillan, Harold Wilson, Margaret Thatcher, and
    Tony Blair.
26. U.S. – Bill Clinton – President

Alumni of Harvard who became Heads of State:
1. Albania – Fan Noli – Prime Minister
2. Bolivia – Eduardo Rodríguez Veltze – President
3. Canada –
   a. William Lyon Mackenzie King – Prime Minister
   b. Pierre Trudeau – Prime Minister
4. Chile – Miguel Juan Sebastián Piñera Echenique – President
5. Colombia – Álvaro Uribe Vélez, President
6. Cook Islands – Thomas Davis, Prime Minister
7. Costa Rica – José María Figueres, President
8. Ecuador – Jamil Mahuad, President
9. Greece – Andreas Papandreou – Prime Minister
10. Hong Kong – Sir Donald Tsang, Chief Executive and Head of Government
11. Ireland Republic of – Mary Robinson, President
12. Jamaica – Edward Seaga – Prime Minister
13. Liberia – Ellen Johnson Sirleaf, President
14. México –
    a. Miguel de la Madrid, President
    b. Carlos Salinas de Gortari, President
    c. Felipe de Jesús Calderón Hinojosa, President
15. Mongolia – Tsakhiagiin Elbegdorj, Prime Minister
16. Norway – Gro Harlem Brundtland, Prime Minister
17. Pakistan – Benazir Bhutto, Prime Minister
18. Singapore – Lee Hsien Loong, Prime Minister
19. South Korea – Syngman Rhee – President
20. Taiwan –
    a. Ma Ying-jeou, President
    b. Annette Lu – Vice President
21. Tanzania – Frederick Sumaye – Prime Minister

22. United States –
   a. Al Gore – Vice President
   b. Barack H. Obama, – President (also First Lady Michelle Obama)
   c. Elbridge Gerry – Vice President
   d. Franklin D. Roosevelt – President
   e. George W. Bush – President
   f. John Adams – President
   g. John F. Kennedy – President
   h. John Quincy Adams – President
   i. Rutherford Hayes – President
   j. Theodore Roosevelt – President

AUTHOR'S contact information:
E-mail: mini4@cox.net

Additional copies of this book are available at:

http://www.winmarkcom.com/powerandprivilege.htm

and by mail from:

**Winmark Communications
17834 N. 41st Ave.
Glendale, AZ 85308**